THE MEANING OF ROUSSEAU

THE MEANING OF ROUSSEAU

ERNEST HUNTER WRIGHT

NEW YORK
RUSSELL & RUSSELL · INC
1963

FIRST PUBLISHED IN 1929
REISSUED, 1963, BY RUSSELL & RUSSELL, INC.
L. C. CATALOG CARD NO: 63—9326

PRINTED IN THE UNITED STATES OF AMERICA

PREFACE

IN this little volume I have tried to put down Rousseau's main opinions as a long perusal of his work has led me to believe he meant them. It is surely time we knew his own intention. After all our years of controversy over him we have still no document in English, and but few in any language, that will simply tell us what he meant to say; and in consequence a great deal of our controversy has been over things he never meant at all. If a statement of his meaning may not still the controversy, it may save us at the least from further tilting at the various men of straw who have sprung up in his image. That is all my reason for attempting it.

I could have tried to do an easier thing. It will soon appear that there are reasons in the nature of our author's utterance, and still others in the nature of the criticism that he has encountered, which will make it hard enough to be sure of his meaning at all points. I may therefore have gone wrong in detail, or even upon fundamentals. If so, I shall be the first to welcome a correction. But I would ask a single word of privilege in this regard before beginning. At several points in the following pages I have shown that there are certain passages in Rousseau, often of a rather startling nature, which remain at real or seeming variance with the fundamental meaning I have found throughout his work. If it were not for these passages, indeed, or rather if it were not for the strange interpretations they have all too often suffered, I should never have begun the present essay, for it would have been unnecessary. And while I am freely open to correction, I am fain to hope I may escape a kind of criticism that has already done too much to cloud our author's meaning by only dressing up a few of his audacious flourishes of rhetoric in the guise of his main doctrine. In the effort to find out his doctrine, I have tried to ponder all his work together. If I am in error, I would ask to have it shown by an appeal to all his utterance rather than to an occasional flash of paradox.

I have pleasure in thanking three of my friendly colleagues, Professor Harry Morgan Ayres, Professor Jefferson Butler Fletcher, and Professor Ashley Horace Thorndike, for reading portions of my manuscript and offering welcome criticism.

E. H. W.

COLUMBIA UNIVERSITY,
20 May 1928.

CONTENTS

I. The Natural Man . . 1

II. The Natural Education . 34

III. The Natural Society . 69

IV. The Natural Religion . 113

Bibliography . . 165

Index . . . 166

Διόπερ πρῶτος ὁ Ζήνων ἐν τῷ Περὶ ἀνθρώπου φύσεως τέλος εἶπε τὸ ὁμολογουμένως τῇ φύσει ζῆν, ὅπερ ἐστὶ κατ' ἀρετὴν ζῆν· ἄγει γὰρ πρὸς ταύτην ἡμᾶς ἡ φύσις.

Diogenes Laertius, vii. 87.

Lo, this only have I found, that God hath made man upright; but they have sought out many inventions.

Ecclesiastes, vii. 29.

I

THE NATURAL MAN

THOUGH the critics have long been busier with our author than with almost any other modern writer, they are still in such dissension as to leave his meaning mainly in the dark. They may have done as ill with other men in former centuries, and for a single instance we may bear in mind how long they managed to keep Aristotle in obscurity and near the verge of travesty. In a similar measure they are now at odds not only on the truth or value of the things that Rousseau said, but even as to what it is he meant to say. And so angry has dissension over him now grown that it is hard to frame a single phrase about his meaning which will be agreeable to all his critics, even as a basis for discussion.

This will be all too apparent as we go on, but a few examples may be given now. Four men out of five will say that when Rousseau tells us to return to nature, he means us to give up all the hard-won gains of culture and get back to savagery or animality. Voltaire implied as much in his ironical confession that Rousseau made him itch to go on all fours ; and down to our day a host of critics far less nimble-jointed have kept finding the same admonition in our author and greeting it with every exhibition of amazement, spleen, or horror. But other critics tell us that Rousseau means no such thing; that he never once says it, but repeatedly denies it; and that far from pleading with us to go back to savagery, he is imploring us to press on to a higher culture than any we have known. Why is it that we read such opposite meanings in him?

Because they both are there, say some of the critics, along with many other opposites; because his work is nothing but a quilt of shreds and patches. One of his books, they say, will contradict another, and one page or passage in a single treatise will annihilate the next. And many a critic throws up his hands when Rousseau gives one kind of education to his chosen pupil but prescribes another for the boys of Poland; when he calls property the root of nearly all our evil and then treats it as a sacred institution; when he pleads for individual liberty and in the same breath for absolute submission to the state; when he preaches tolerance for all men and banishes the atheists from his republic; when he is a proud aristocrat and a pernicious leveller, a reformer looking only backward and a revolutionist afraid to take the first step forward, and a dozen other inconsistent things by fits and starts. To list all of the inconsistencies that have been found in him would at least help us to see how he can be called the father of so many movements in our modern world, however inconsistent these may be in turn. Surely twenty times as many have been traced to him as to any other modern man; but if we can only prove him contradictory enough, we may put them all down to his blame or credit. Yet there are critics with such names as Höffding and Lanson who assure us that Rousseau's work is all a unity, with or without superficial contradictions, that he had a single thought at heart, and that no one but a hasty reader need be led astray by his incidental or apparent inconsistencies. What is it that leaves us in this clash about his meaning?

Or did he have a veritable meaning? Did he own the kind of brain that generates what we call thought? Morley says that Rousseau never rose to 'the distinction of knowing how to think,'[1] in any proper sense, though he indulged a lower form of cerebral performance so important as to ask for ample criticism. But Faguet calls him a 'prodigious thinker'[2] in a book entitled *Rousseau Penseur*. As a biographer of Burke, Morley knew well that Burke assailed Rousseau largely for his reliance upon logic to clear up the troubles of humanity, and with all its perils logic still passes for a form of thought. But though many a man like Lowell[3] has called Rousseau a rigorous logician, many another has answered with Dunning[4] that we may as well try to 'visualize the fauna of the Apocalypse' as to follow Rousseau's logic. In Morley's mind the answer that Burke gave to Rousseau's 'valueless' speculations is the 'greatest, widest, and loftiest' utterance of all time upon the

[1] *Rousseau*, i. 89.   [2] *Rousseau Penseur*, p. 408.
[3] *Literary Essays*, London, 1890, ii. 245.
[4] *Political Science Quarterly*, xxiv. 3, 385.

issues at stake;[1] in Vaughan's mind it is indeed a 'masterpiece', but still 'immeasurably inferior' to Rousseau's reasoning 'in practical insight, in breadth and wisdom'. For Vaughan finds Rousseau 'richer in speculative ideas than any man of his century',[2] excepting only Kant. And Kant too felt a 'rare penetration of mind' in our author.[3]

Under each of these banners, and still others, troops a little legion of the critics. What is there in Rousseau's brain to set them at such odds? How is it that Immanuel Kant, to name no other, found in Rousseau's pages the sole thing that ever kept him from the famous promenade that people set their clocks by, when men like Lemaître and Lasserre, like Seillière and Nourrisson, can see little or nothing in them but clashing phantasms in the guise of reason and a deadly virus oozing from a sick soul in lieu of moral principle? Why is it so hard to see what Rousseau means?

It is not because his utterance is thick. If there is one thing that the critics all admit in him, it is lucidity of style. Nor is it because his matter is abstruse. He labours harder than any other philosopher to avoid metaphysical contortion and to write what any reading man may read. Yet he is still at fault for some of our troubles with him. A poet and a philosopher at once, in a period when poetry was about as nearly dead, at least in his own tongue, as it had ever been since the Dark Ages, and when philosophy was about as identical with science as it had ever been since Thales, he may have chafed more than he knew at the narrow terms in vogue for either, and he certainly failed to fuse the two in perfect unity. Every so often the poet in him traverses the philosopher to our confusion. Possibly the rhetorician does still worse. For Rousseau has the dubious gift of epigram, and loves to fling off now and then a kind of paradox that remains unforgettable when all the context that explains and mitigates it is forgotten. Thus every one remembers his saying that 'the man who meditates is a degenerate animal;'[4] and only too often that paradox and a few others like it have been taken

---

[1] Op. cit., ii. 191, 192.
[2] C. E. Vaughan, The Political Writings of Rousseau, i. 83, 93.
[3] Ed. Hartenstein, 1867, viii. 624.
[4] Œuvres, i. 87. Unless otherwise indicated, all references are to the Hachette edition.

for the head and front of his philosophy. Even so it may remain a question whether the main fault is with an author who will mar his meaning with such paradox or with a critic who will wrest the paradox out of its context for the glory of inferring that it is all the author meant. But there is more to say. The thought of Rousseau is by no means one of those rare systems all laid out minutely in advance, with every item in precise position and in perfect harmony with all the others. It grew and gathered in his reveries like a flowing river, fed by many tributaries as it struggled to its outlet. And its unity, if such it has, is like that of a swelling stream. If we are looking for such unity, we must be prepared for ebb and flood, for twists and turns, for cross-currents, eddies, and backwaters, with possibly a whirlpool here and there; and we may have trouble to make sure that the main current goes in one direction.

Rousseau might have saved us some of the trouble if he had drawn up a little brief of his first principles. Of course he gives us all of them in scattered passages, but the trials of his critics are enough to show that these are not always easy to assemble. He might have spared us trouble if he had always used the same term in precisely the same sense, or had allowed for any variation. He could have spared us a good deal, at moments when he was inexorably pushing logic on disparate problems to conclusions equally disparate, if he had admitted the discrepancies and shown a reason for them, and a higher unity when possible. He is by no means the only man who has encountered such disparities. We have had no greater thinkers than the men who argue that slavery is desirable for a community but undesirable for an individual, that God is impossible in one kind of reason but necessary in another kind, and many similar 'contradictions'. Most of the contradictions in Rousseau likewise arise in passing from one universe of discourse to another, but it would have been well for him to say so in the act. Thus he could easily have said that the first man who seized a piece of property may have brought a host of evils on the world, but that in the ideal commonwealth the ownership of such property as the law legitimizes may still be a sacred and beneficent right. Possibly he thought he did say it, or did not need to say it; but the quarrels of the critics seem to prove that he should have taken greater pains. So in these and other ways Rousseau is partly at fault for our dissensions.

But he is not mainly so, for the main fault lies indubitably with his critics. He has been a problem for more kinds of comment than almost any other man, for he invades so many fields of thought that literary critics, anthropologists, sociologists, economists, political scientists, educators, moralists, metaphysicians, theologians of every faith, psychologists old and new, physicians to the mind or body, and other specialists in profusion have all felt they had to reckon with him. And there has been a vast confusion of tongues. Thus his idea of the natural man, basic as it is for all his thinking, may well mean one thing to the anthropologist who takes this man for the first human being of all time, another to the psychologist who thinks of him as the essential man of any time, and yet another to the moralist who may look upon him as the last man still to come and wear the crown of all our culture. Which of these did Rousseau mean? And so with many of his other ideas; when we speak so many languages about him, we are sure to disagree. And the temptation then is to simplify our troubles by putting our own label on him and forgetting all else about him —by tagging him once for all as the high-priest of nature, or the first 'cosmopolitan', or the 'man of feeling', or the father of the Revolution, or the maker of Romanticism, and then resting from thought in deference to the phrase. A good book [1] is written to show the Anglicism of Rousseau, and for a time it is all but enough to call him a Septentrional. A very bad one [2] is published to assure us that Rousseau is Romanticism and Romanticism is Rousseau, and a little coterie of monarchists find in its florid style and fustian logic about all that it is polite to know about him. The trouble with such phrases is that they tear the author piecemeal, and let the part conceal the whole. If we are to find his meaning we must take him altogether— take him simply as one more philosopher struggling with nearly every problem in a century full of them.

But the worst thing is still to say. The main reason why we have not found out the truth about Rousseau is simply that we

[1] Texte, *Jean-Jacques Rousseau et les origines du cosmopolitisme littéraire.*
[2] Lasserre, *Le Romantisme français.*

have not *wanted* to find it. We have wanted only to glorify him, or far oftener to vilify him, and neither thing is possible for any one who knows him. Nearly all men have seen red at his name. There are familiar reasons for it. Rousseau is not a pleasant man, for one thing, though there may be good in him. For another, he goes straight to the root of all that is vital to us, and incidentally tears the mask away from many a dear prejudice as he looks into our schools, our governments, our morals, our religion, and our very nature. He raises such a storm within us that very few of us have been able to keep our heads in reading him. So among the thousands of books about him there are few indeed that are impartial or truly critical. The vast number are campaign documents; they resemble nothing quite so much as the outpour of pamphleteering we expect in any hot political campaign. And we need scarcely look for the truth in them, for even if intended it is stifled in the heated air. If we can fancy a celestial visitor arriving in the midst of one of our most turbulent campaigns and trying to find out the sober truth about the candidates and issues by faithfully perusing every utterance of the press from communistic to reactionary, we shall have a very fair notion of the plight of any novice starting with the critics of Rousseau.

This is not agreeable to say. It is not a pleasant thing to feel that the net result of all the criticism of five generations has been to cloud our author's meaning rather than to clarify it, and that the people of his own time understood him better because the critics had hardly started to explain him. But such appears to be the fact. If so, it may seem rather bold to try once more to say what Rousseau means; and yet it may not be supremely hard to grasp his meaning if we can but keep our heads and seek all aid from the few impartial critics who have cleared the way. If we fall into passing errors, we may possibly hope to get the main truths clear. And they are important for us, for they reach the root of nearly every problem of our troubled day.

I

Nature is right. If we will take the words as Rousseau meant them, we shall have a key to all he has to say. But if we fall into the easy error of starting with a meaning for them all our own, we shall hardly come to know what he intended. And since few words invite more variant interpretations, we shall need a certain self-control if we are simply to lay open his own meaning, for what it may avail, in the rest of our chapter. To that end we may set aside at once a few things which he does not mean.

He does not mean, as commonly supposed, that animal desire is our only guide. Such an idea was all too prevalent around him. It inspired Saint-Lambert to raise his glass to 'The return to nature and the morals of Otaheite'.[1] It lay back of Diderot's assertion that all our trouble comes from the fact that there was once a natural man into whose skin we have crammed an artificial man, with constant civil war for a result between the two, and that the only way out is to set the natural man at liberty again.[2] It appears in many another place; and no wonder if we find an occasional passage in Rousseau as well which may be read to the same purpose. But it is quite alien to the main spirit of his work, for this is a long protest against such a philosophy. To say no more at present, it is not possible that the man who tried to train a boy through rigorous control to self-control of equal rigour, or who demanded absolute submission from his citizens to the state, should have merely meant to gratify desire in the boy or the citizens. Nature is right because nature is more than desire, because conscience and reason are its better part, as we shall find, and are appointed to control desire. So we may go ahead in the assurance that there is no intent to call desire and duty the same thing.

Nor does he mean, as often thought, that nature is all one for man and brute. The air around him was fairly full of the idea that all our acts are as automatic as the responses of an animal to stimulus or of a stone to gravity; but this again is what aroused Rousseau to his revolt. The nature of man is one,

---

[1] *Mémoires de Madame d'Épinay*, ed. Boiteau, i. 216.
[2] *Supplément au voyage de Bougainville*, ed. Assézat, ii. 246.

and that of brute and stone is other; and what sets man apart, as we shall duly see, is above all a freedom of action that is his alone. Nature is right again because she has given man to know a certain liberty; so we may proceed without the fear that we shall end with a single law for man and thing.

Neither does he mean that the only way to be natural is to be a savage. This was also a familiar notion in his circle, and the irony of criticism has chosen him for its one apostle in all time. Yet he never said it. He never meant that there was long ago a natural man in the person of our earliest forbear and that there has been no other since, or that there is one in every cradle who begins to vanish with the first lesson from its elders. Of course the infant and the savage are natural enough, in a sense at once intelligible though by no means enviable, but they enjoy no monopoly of nature. The adult and the citizen may be natural too. In fact, the infant and the savage cannot remain natural if they stay in infancy and savagery, for it is in their nature to outgrow these. They can remain natural only by growing up; and since growing up implies perpetual change, they may be natural at any point only as they vary more or less with every point they reach. The natural man may thus live in any time or place, but will vary with the time and place he lives in, just as the unnatural man may live at any time except of course at the first moment of his being. But at the extreme poles the natural savage will be about as different from the natural citizen as a natural infant from a natural adult. There is a vast difference between a natural man in the state of nature and a natural man in the civil state.

Then what is it that remains the same in all these changes? And how may we stay natural at every point, or become unnatural at any?

Allowing fully for all obvious differences, we may be clearest if we start with a comparison between a natural man and a natural specimen of a simpler order. In one sense, every tree in the forest is altogether natural—in the sense that it has simply grown of its own will, without our interference. But in another sense no one of them is fully natural—in the sense that every one of them is more or less impeded by untoward conditions from arriving at the full development of its own nature to which it is evermore aspiring. Now we may take a given tree and merely offer it every aid of space and soil and sunshine to fulfil its aspiration. It will be an ampler tree through our art, but still an altogether natural one in that it has grown only in accord with its own principle. We have only helped it to perfect its nature. Or we may do a very different thing. We may make it into something it would never be of its own motion—may pollard it into a tufted pole, trim it to the shape of a pyramid or peacock, force it to grow slantwise or horizontally, or bend it to a thousand purposes alien to its principle. Then it is no longer a natural tree; our art has but denatured it. Even so our art may do with man, and far more also; as much more as his capacity for cultivation is greater than the tree's. There is an art that leaves him natural, to whatever height of culture it may lift him; nay, that makes him the more natural, so to say, in aiding him to the perfection of his nature. And there is an art that only denatures him. So the conflict is not between nature and art, but only between nature and the second kind of art.

Here we begin to see what Rousseau does mean. If nature is right, all the art that aids us to fulfil her purposes is also right, and any art that urges us to other ends is wrong. The original germ of nature in us is the test of all our art. That germ resides in every one of us, and in the infant and the savage too ; only the infant is like an acorn that may one day be an oak, and the savage like some primitive shrub that may in time evolve into an oak. It is in the nature of infant and savage to grow up into man and citizen just as it is in the nature of acorn and shrub to develop into oaks. One of the processes is more or less conscious, of course, while the other is all unconscious, and there are many other differences between them; so we are comparing them, so far as is allowable, merely for the sake of clarity. Now we have three choices open to us as we watch the processes. We may simply leave nature alone, and let acorn and shrub take their chance of growing into the amplest oak they may, or child and savage into the amplest man and citizen. But we can make an ampler oak, and a far ampler man and citizen, through the kind of art we have called right. Or we may make distorted oaks, and equally distorted men, by

the art we have called wrong. In these choices Rousseau does
not hesitate. He is for the right art.

So he means that we may continue natural through all the
changes in our growth if every change is in accordance with the
principle of our own being at the start and thus receives its
sanction, but that we become unnatural in so far as any change
goes counter to that primal principle. If we cling to the path
thus charted for us we may climb what cultural heights we
please and still remain in nature, but the moment we forsake it
we have gone astray. This is hardly startling, and indeed it
runs the risk of sounding like a truism; for it really comes to
saying that we are natural as long as we are true to our own
nature. But it is still about the opposite of what nearly all the
world thinks Rousseau meant, and equally the opposite of
what he thought nearly all the world was bent on doing. For
if it is easy to announce his principle, it is difficult indeed to live
up to it. There is nothing harder than to keep true to our
nature as he would have us do it; and that is why he thinks
that there may have never been a natural man, and that there
may never be one. But if ever there is one, he will be the man
who has not strayed. And he will not need to be a savage;
rather he will have to be the best of all philosophers.

Now it is only fair to state that there are passages in Rousseau that do not say this, though far more that say it quite
explicitly; but there are passages, few though often striking,
that even seem to say the contrary. And it is all too tempting
to tear them out of the main body of the work and so make
them mean something more amazing than what we have been
saying—make them mean that nature is eternal savagery and
that all art is pernicious. It has been a favourite pastime to do
this. But surely we have now failed long enough to see the
forest for these few ill-sorted trees. Surely we need not go on
saying that in the effort of a thousand pages to make Emile into
a natural man our author is only bent on keeping him a Hotten-
tot, or that in the endeavour to set up an ideal republic he
craves nothing better than a horde of naked savages to serve
as citizens. But this is what we shall have to say if we go on believing that Rousseau had nothing but a savage in his mind
when he spoke of the natural man; and the notion is so pre-

posterous that it may now be relegated to burlesque, which has
always been its proper home.

And lest the idea that the natural man is simply any man
who always keeps the faith with his own primal nature should
sound too much like a truism, we may pause a moment, before
pursuing it to unexpected ends, to say that we nearly always
act upon its opposite. Deep down in most of our hearts lurks a
conviction that the nature of man is more or less desperately
wicked, and that the aim of all our art is to rescue him from
natural iniquity. For many a prophet and philosopher has told
us this. Perhaps the Sage of Malmesbury is the high-priest of
the creed; nature is about as wrong as may be, and the right art
is to suppress her. Doubtless Rousseau is the major prophet
of the other dispensation; nature is the test of all our art, and
the right art is to perfect her. So the right art is all his study;
and since it issues from the very nature of man, our primal
nature is his first quest. If his faith is no truism, if indeed it led
him into paths heretical enough to bring him exile, what
reasons can he give for holding it?

He may well have found the germ of it by simply looking
at the sorry part that he and others played in the corruption of
the day and wondering whether they had fallen into so much
evil mainly in obedience to their nature or mainly in defiance of
it. Were their sins and errors mostly relics of a primal nature
still at work in them, or were they the issue of an art gone contrary to it? Are we born as evil as we have now grown, or are
we born more evil still and is our present state a great if in-
complete reform? The question comes to most of us from
time to time. In a terrible convulsion, for example, which sets
half the good men of the world blowing one another into atoms
on the battlefield, we can hardly fail to wonder whether we are
suffering from some uprush of an instinct in our nature to tear
and scratch, or whether possibly we have fallen into such a
tangle of our art that we can see no way out except one that
puts our very nature to the blush. 'God called them and found
them worthy of Him' reads an inscription over the soldiers
lying in a certain green churchyard. It is no reflection on their
valour or their pure intention to wonder whether God made
them for Verdun and looked down with some inscrutable

delight upon them there; or whether only a tangle in our art of statecraft is here celebrated by a tangle in our science of theology. Rousseau saw a sight about as dismal as our war: a host of decadent men and women drunk with dancing on the tremulous lid of revolution. And since these men and women were surely products of the highest art, he could hardly keep from wondering whether they were so mad and evil mainly in spite of it or mainly because of it. Were their virtues all given them by an art which had in so far suppressed their nature, and were their vices only lingerings of a nature which their art had not yet been able to eliminate? Rousseau saw no reason for thinking so ill of our birthright.

But this is not yet argument. It is a guess, or at the most a faith; and if any one guess otherwise, Rousseau can hardly argue with him until he has more evidence to go on. He can hardly appeal to religion by declaring that if our nature is all wrong God must have made an error, for that only raises the worst problem in all religion. Nor can he well have recourse to bare logic in the assertion that if we are to stamp out our very nature we shall be at endless war with our own selves, in endless struggle to break down the principle of our own being; for if the very principle is desperately wicked, we must do what we can to uproot it. So the only course for Rousseau is to try to find proof for his first assertion that our primal nature is good, and so show what he means by saying that nature is right; and to that end he must now tell us just what he thinks our primal nature is. That is why it is his first quest.

It is not an easy one. So muffled are we all in the folds on folds of culture which our arts have woven around us that it is hard indeed to peer through and descry the vital germ of nature hidden and often all but smothered underneath. The only way to look for it is to strip off every vesture that can possibly have been the gift of art until we come to something which no art can have given us and which we must therefore take as native to us. Such at least was Rousseau's way of searching, or the way invented for him by his predecessors; and in common with many of them he comes first to two things which he must suppose original in our nature.

The first thing is self-love (*amour de soi*), or what we now call the instinct of self-preservation. This must have been natural to man, or he would have perished at the start. And it cannot but be good, for every one at least except the plenary pessimist who believes that the best thing for the race would have been to perish with its birth.

The second thing is sympathy (*pitié*), or what we call the gregarious instinct or the instinct of mutual aid. For we have found out the important part the instinct played, within a given species, in mitigating the rigour of the struggle for survival. Sympathy must also have been natural, for if men had been more intent on mutual harm than mutual help they would soon have killed off one another. And it is also good, for every one but the same pessimist.[1]

These two instincts are the root of all our being, and all else in us must grow or be engrafted on them. They abide in every man, and indeed in many other creatures. For the love of self is found in all the animals, and the love of kind in many of them; so man must wait a moment longer for a trait that is his own alone. The instincts are obviously prior to all reason in us. And though they are obviously good, they have yet no sort of claim to be called moral, for a moral act is one that is directed to an end foreseen in reason. But we may be good before we can be moral, for goodness may be antecedent to morality even as is instinct to reflection. We are good in the beginning because our earliest instincts bring more help than harm to us and to our fellows. In so far did Rousseau mean that man is good by nature, and only in so far did he ever mean the famous doctrine, so often understood to claim illimitably more. In one sense it is a very modest claim; it was the tiniest of sops to the apostles of the Noble Savage among whom our author is erroneously supposed to be the chief. But in

---

[1] With no essential change in meaning, Rousseau wavers somewhat as to the exact relations between the two instincts of *amour de soi* and *pitié*. In the *Discourse on Inequality* they are equally primal to us; in *Emile, pitié* has become the first immediate derivative from the *amour de soi*. But their office is the same. The change was doubtless made to placate and refute at once the reigning philosophy that nothing whatever is natural to us except self-love; Rousseau is quite willing to agree to that if he can show, as he attempts, that self-love will immediately engender sympathy. The terms were international commonplaces in the century; see the *Essay on Man*, for instance. (And reflect in passing on the thinness of such literary partitions as would shut off the worlds of Pope and Rousseau so completely. For all his modernity, Rousseau was probably quite as near to the century of Racine as to that of Hugo.)

another sense the modest claim is most important. For whether man is mainly good or noxious by his nature will soon make a vast difference in our dealings with him; nearly every item in his education, for one thing, will depend upon the answer. And Rousseau does emphatically mean that Hobbes and all the rest who think that man is fundamentally noxious have misread his earliest instincts and gone wrong from the beginning.

Though evidently good so far, the two instincts are bound to come into some conflict. Self-love will crave everything for self, but sympathy will have to cede something to others; and in the conflict will arise our earliest quandary in conduct. It is not a moral problem yet, for the reason given, but it is at least a dilemma in desires. Of all the forms in which it might arise in primitive days, the easiest for us to imagine is perhaps the quandary of any parent who desires what he knows his infants also need, and in this form, as probably in others, it may come to many an animal inferior to man. We may possibly conceive the crisis in the breast of some poor robin with a worm upon its tongue but with nestlings who are hungry too, and we may even wonder what tragedies the groves have seen during a slack season in worms. But not to travesty the idea, we can see that our instinct to crave everything for self must learn to make peace with our instinct to get along with others, and that there must be continual compromise between the two. And out of the constant compromise in which our instincts learn to supplement and mitigate each other, and to work in harmony, is born the all-important sentiment to which we give the name of conscience. This is the very first derivative of our two instincts. It is therefore no mere product of education, no fabric woven out of a thousand admonitions about right and wrong; it is older than all education, and a simple gift of nature. Older than our reason, it is not a moral thing as yet, as we have seen, but it is all-important because it is the only basis on which reason can ever build morality, the only gift that will ever make us willing to be moral. Conscience is natural to man, and once more the nature of man is good.

But conscience is blind. It is nothing but a sentiment; and whether or not it was alone sufficient for the simple problems of primeval man, it is quite inadequate in the perplexities that

now assail us. The sole guide for conscience amid these perplexities is the faculty of reason that develops with them. In
our present complications reason alone can show us, with that
species of demonstration of which finite minds are capable,
that one thing is right and another wrong. Reason alone can
make us moral by ordering action to determined ends, can
shape a principle or give a meaning to the word 'duty'. Reason
alone can fashion our natural goodness into virtue. But she
can do no more. She can show us right and wrong, but she has
no power to move us to the love of right or to the hatred of
wrong. Conscience only can do that ; only by our inborn
sentiment are we moved to love the right and hate the wrong
that reason sets apart for us. Without reason we should never
know them, and without conscience we should rest indifferent
to them. Conscience is the moral force, reason the moral guide.

If Rousseau writes more paeans to conscience than to reason
there are several causes for it. The main one is simply that
conscience was all out of fashion in his day, for nearly all the
thinkers in his circle were contemptuously denying that there
was such a thing. Striving to restore it to a place in thought, he
naturally pressed its claims; and reason had slight need of
similar panegyric. For another thing, he thought it of more
ancient lineage than reason, and entitled to whatever honour was
accordant. And in one sense at least he also felt it was infallible;
in the sense that conscience cannot of necessity but love the
right, and has no way of loving wrong, though of course it may
be terribly misled to mistake the two. But he felt reason to be
very fallible, and thought he saw the wrecks of it all around
him; he thought the reasoners of his day were very frequently
misleading conscience into love of wrong disguised as right.
Even so he has his eulogies for reason too, and it may be said
in passing that no man who gives reason the sole office of
deciding between right and wrong can well be called, as Rousseau often is, an anti-rationalist. We shall meet quite as much
reasoning in him, whether mainly right or wrong, as in any
one who was writing in his language at the time. It is not anti-
rational to believe that reasoners make errors, and that is all
his charge against them as such. Nor is it anti-rational to think
that conscience is older than reason in us, whether that be true

or not; or to argue that virtue can result only from a perfect union of the two.

But in a perfect union neither party may go on his own sweet way. Of course all our prior sentiment must now look to reason for guidance into culture; but reason in turn must begin by validating all the antecedent sentiment as proper to us and as the only basis on which she can build the culture that is right. Her first discovery must be that this is the sole rational thing to do. And the errors that Rousseau thought he saw in the reasoners of his day were two—either they denied a part of our primal nature and reared an unsound culture on the other part alone, or they ignored it all and pried around for something else entirely to build on. The one group held that self-love was our nature whole and entire, and so built a culture with no other basis than pure selfishness and with no morality except design-ing prudence. The other group simply insisted on building a culture which nothing in our nature would countenance. To use the homeliest illustration, Rousseau felt they might as well be trying to make dolphins fly and eagles swim; they would never really gain their end, but they might do grievous injury by the way. Even such injury he felt they had done to many a man around him, and even so he thought reason must always do when she flies off from the verities of our primal nature and fares forth into fantasies of her own dreaming. As long as she ignores the native form of man, she can be only an irre-sponsible fashioner of new fangles that will never fit him. And this is the real anti-rationalism. The truer reason is responsible; and the rational thing is to limit reason to the plain facts of the rest of our nature. She will still have an ample part to play. So Rousseau is far from rejecting reason but also far from giving her illimitable sway. He sees safety only in a perfect union in which sentiment and reason mutually check and con-trol each other—in which sentiment urges reason to the right path, and in which reason leads us along it toward perfection.

Now we may put all this historically, as we have doubtless done in several phrases. We may say that far back in the past man started with a blend of sentiments for all his nature, and that through the ages reason has been clothing him in the cul-ture he has now inherited; the doctrine would then mean that reason has done well in so far as she has shaped the clothing to the man. But Rousseau is not much interested in this kind of history, and such is not his usual way of speaking. Only once did he indulge it at large, in the *Discourse on Inequality* where the question he was answering forced him into the conjectural history of man from naked savagery onward. Or we may put it all another way. We may let the savage go, and simply say that every one of us comprises that same blend of sentiments, around which reason has woven her fabric of culture; and that reason has done well again in so far as she has respected those elemental sentiments. Such is Rousseau's usual way of speaking in maturer works like *Emile* and the *Social Contract*, though he sometimes mingles the two methods.

Then where is the natural man, in either process? He may be anywhere along the line. He may be the naked savage or he may be any later man in whom reason has kept the elemental sentiments intact; while the unnatural man will be one in whom she has distorted or suppressed them. It may possibly be better to be any sort of natural man, however rude, than an unnatural one, however cultivated; better to be an ignorant savage than a perverted philosopher. Ignorance is preferable to error. But that is not the only choice; and it is infinitely better to be the final natural man than to be the earliest, to be a true philosopher rather than a barbarian. So once more the natural man of Rousseau's admiration is not a savage. Rather he is Cato; or rather he is the kind of man that Cato tried to be. To try to be that man in due time is the nature of us all, if we will only let it grow aright.

Then why is it that most of us are not that, and do not even want to be it? If man is good, how have men grown bad? Made up of self-love and sympathy, with conscience for a first gift, we were meant to be good; and we waited upon reason to lift us up to virtue. But somewhere in the process we seem to have gone wrong. When did we stray?

When we let self-love swell up into pride, Rousseau would answer; and the two things are as different for him as the natural flesh from a swollen tumour. Self-love (*amour de soi*) is good so long as it simply satisfies our needs, for not to do so cannot but be bad. But the moment it lures us beyond our need into comparisons between our lot and that of some one else, the moment it tempts us to vainglory in securing more than others, or to envy for the opposite reason, it has degenerated into pride (*amour-propre*). Now it is not very hard to supply our real needs, for they are simple. And even though two of us may need a single thing which only one of us can have, we need not go beyond self-love in dealing for it. If we are civilized, we may each urge the other to take it, in a social courtesy which may rest ultimately on the natural sympathy of which we spoke. If we are savage, we shall doubtless proceed with scanter ceremony. In either case the one who takes the thing is so far acting from self-love, and the other is simply out of fortune but may hope for better luck next time; neither is at fault so far. But if the lucky one should turn and scorn his fellow for his inability to get the thing, he has fallen into pride and is engendering it in his companion. He has already satisfied his true need and is now conjuring up a false one in the unholy joy of making his fellow feel the poorer. This is all the difference there is between self-love and pride, but we have only to look at our envious world to see how monstrous it has grown.

Self-love will seek only what we need; pride will tend to snatch at everything, whether needed or not, for the evil pleasure of having more than some one else, more if possible than anybody else—the evil pleasure, in the last analysis, of humiliating some one. Self-love leaves us in peace when our wants are satisfied; pride keeps us for ever hungry for the adulation of others, until we come to live our very lives in their opinions. Self-love is satiable, for our true needs are limited; pride is insatiable, for the false needs we can conjure up are numberless. Self-love is primal and natural, pride is secondary and artificial. It is the mother of all evil. In the form of avarice it gloats in more riches than another has, or grieves in less. In the form of despotism it rejoices over slaves and subjects. In the form of vanity it lives upon the breath of those who may profess to feel inferior. In every form it finds its joy in another's pain, its pain in another's joy, whether its name be jealousy, spite, ambition, vengeance, hatred, fraud, or any other vice. These are the sins of men, and every one of them is born of pride.

It is instantly objected that the distinction between self-love
and pride is a pure fiction. There is no such thing as self-love
apart from pride, for the one immediately begets the other;
or rather the two are the upper and the under sides of the same
plane, are one and the same thing. If we are to love ourselves
we cannot but prefer ourselves to others, with all the comparisons involved. So pride is just as natural to us as self-love, and
we are therefore good and bad from the beginning.

Will the objection hold? Perhaps not entirely; perhaps
hardly at all. If we say that pride is natural to us, we must base
the assertion either on history or on logic, or on both. If on
history, we mean that in the crepuscular day when human
beings first appeared, pride was already part and parcel of self-
love in them. If on logic, we mean that it is not possible to
separate self-love from pride in thought, because they are one
identical thing under two names.

In answer to the argument from history, Rousseau bids us
think a moment about the first troop of men that ever drew
together. They were certainly strong in self-love; they were
bent on their true needs exclusively. The needs were simple
and could probably be easily satisfied; but easily or not, they
could be satisfied only by each man toiling for himself. Then
what did these men want of one another? Nothing at all, or
next to nothing. But that is to say that they had little or no
pride. And yet it must have happened that one of them would
snatch a morsel or a mate from another? Certainly, and let us
call that a show of pride if so we must; though for Rousseau it
is far more like the thing he calls self-love. For he reminds us
that these men were merely animals, and that their thieveries
were committed solely or all but solely for the satisfaction of
their needs, and hardly if at all for the humiliation of their
victims. When a dog fights for a bone he has little or nothing
but self-love to instigate him; he can have but slight intent, if
any, to shame the other dog, for intent to shame is born of
more reflection. And we ourselves should scarcely feel humi-
liated out in the wilds if a lion or a Bushman stole our dinner.
We might be sorry in proportion to our hunger, but we
should hardly suffer in our pride, for there has been no purpose
to put us to shame; so we should take the loss as a sort of

natural event, much as if a flood had carried off the meal. In about the same way our author thinks our earliest forbears must have borne their losses, with a feeling that can hardly be called wounded pride; for pride is injured, not by loss, but only by ridicule. But without insisting on the last letter of these details, he would say that self-love was obviously very strong in the first men and has remained about constant to our day, but that pride was very weak in them, or altogether wanting, and has since swollen to a monstrous size. And so he feels safe in calling the one primal and natural, and the other its secondary form and artificial.

For the logical argument, Rousseau asks us to remember how we found the natural man in logic. We tore off every shred of culture in the quest for what must have been native to us. We could not take away self-love, for we cannot live without it; but we can take away all pride, because it is not necessary to us. We can live quite well without flouting or deriding one another; the pastime is not in the least necessary to our existence. And there is no point in arguing that we all indulge in it, and have long done so, for that is only a renewed appeal to history and has just been heard. Logic simply tells us that we cannot do without self-love, but can do very well without pride; a great deal better without it. And the two can hardly be identical if one is essential to our being and the other not only inessential but inimical to us. Of course one of them grows out of the other, as we have seen, but that is anything but saying that they are the same, even though we may not always know precisely where the one ends and the other begins. The tumour grows out of the natural flesh, and we may never know exactly where it starts, but we can feel it all too painfully.

Is the objection overruled? There would hardly seem to be a great deal of it left—at least far too little to gainsay the evidence that the tumour of pride has been swelling through the ages into the great corruption of our flesh. It is our one chronic disorder, and the parent of all others; and we are all invaded by it, all infirm and all unhappy. What can we do about it?

The answer is as easy as the act is hard. We can give up pride. We can cease from all comparison with other men and simply go about our destiny. We can renounce a host of ima-

ginary needs and hold fast to the true things needful; cast away
a world of illusion and rediscover our own self. We can be
meek, and inherit our soul. In a word, we can *return to nature.*
That is all the famous phrase means.

But all this is old? It is older than the Gospel; Rousseau
only gave it a new life for a people who had come about as near
forgetting it as any we have known. But it is impossible? The
golden rule is impossible; any ideal is impossible, or it would
be no ideal. We have said that there may have never been a
natural man, that there may never be one. Then this natural
man who never existed is only an abstraction? Precisely; the
'natural man' and the 'nature of man' are the same thing, and
both are abstractions. They may never have been perfectly
embodied in an actual man, but they are what an actual man
should try to be. But why not simply call him the ideal man,
and leave out all the disputation about nature? Because we
have no way of finding the ideal for any being without first
discovering his native bent and aptitude, without first asking
of his nature what his end should be. But this ideal is all wrong!
This thing denounced as pride has really been the lever of all
progress, and its truer name is courage, strength, achievement.
With all its evils, it is what has brought us up out of the brutes.
Straight back to them is where the pernicious doctrine of renunciation will carry us; and its true name is anaemia! Many
men have thought so, and most of them would seem to think so
now. Nietzsche for one thinks so, and burnishes up his own
pride in passing by branding Rousseau as a moral tarantula.
Probably exceeding few men really believe in being meek.
But we can hardly risk decision on the question here; it would
take another book, and here we are not trying to prove Rousseau right or wrong so much as to say merely what he means.
Of course he would answer that self-love is quite enough to
keep us from returning to the brutes, and that pride can do no
better; that at the best pride can only mingle sin with progress,
and that at the worst it may degrade us below the very brutes
we are despising. And there we may leave the argument for
whoso cares to ponder it, with the assurance that it raises the
question of questions about Rousseau's doctrine.

II

The doctrine so far is that man begins as a blend of certain sentiments which make for good and which wait for reason to uplift them into culture; and that reason does her work aright when she respects those prior sentiments as the basis and continuous control of all her operations, but only wanders about in realms of fantasy when she ignores or defies them. Though a late-comer to us, reason is of course as natural for us as any of our other gifts, and she has the high office of guide to all the rest. That the others can but stray in blindness if they decline her guidance is so evident that Rousseau scarcely needs to say it, but that reason herself can but fly off into fantasy if she forgets the kind of creature she is guiding and merely plies her art regardless of its ends seemed to him to need more emphasis in an age so given up to reasoning as a sort of sleight-of-hand for sleight-of-hand's sake.

Round the naked germ of our nature reason has now woven the vast and complicated web of culture that makes up man as we behold him. What shall we say of him in her apparel?

No one will say that he has lost nothing in donning it. It is bound to be a harness, and may at worst become a straight-jacket; at least he cannot wear it without losing some of his brute freedom. Once he knew no more restraint than a wild animal, and now he is restricted by a thousand social ties. Once he was absolute and independent like an integer, now he is relative and like the numerator of a fraction whose denominator is the mass of other men who depend on him and on whom he depends. Once he gave his will immediate expression, now he is inhibited and frustrated. So there is no use in feigning that he has suffered no loss. The only question is whether 'other gifts have followed, for such loss, I would believe, abundant recompense'. Now there are too many moments when Rousseau feels the loss like any wild thing caged, feels it far more poignantly than most of us in those moods when we long for a green isle all our own where we can work our will. They are not his admirable moments, and are not his thinking moments. When he is thinking he answers that those other gifts, according to their use, may be blessings or curses. They may be abused, and have been, to worse ends than we could possibly have entertained before we had them; but they can be used, and should be, for ends that bring the most abundant recompense for any loss that may have come with their acquirement.

'Although man loses in the civil state certain advantages which he enjoyed in the state of nature, he gains others so great ... that if the abuses of his new condition did not often degrade him below his former one, he must needs bless unceasingly the happy moment that delivered him from it forever.'[1]

So the question is only one of the use and the abuse of culture.

No one will say that every use of culture has been good. We all loathe some of its performances, though we may not always hit upon the same ones. No one will say that any single gift of culture is above abuse. The simplest of our arts may be made to serve the vilest ends. Speech has been so much misused as to inspire the witticism that it was given us for the concealment of our thought. Writing has often been employed for fraud, and reasoning to make the worse appear the better cause. We are all agreed that any art or science may be plied for either good or evil, and the question whether art and science have been mainly good or evil for us is simply the question whether we have used them or abused them most. So Rousseau must tell us just what constitutes their use and their abuse, and thus give us the test of right and wrong.

This would seem enough, but he must do still more in the same breath. He must even show us, to be true to his first principle, that only the proper use of culture is natural to us, and that its abuse is contrary to our very nature. For he has said these three things: that nature is right, that nature leads us into culture, but that culture is right or wrong according to its usage. And the three can go together only if he can show that our nature bids us make the right use of our culture and avoid its abuse. But many men have said that it is our own evil nature to misuse our gifts, and that nothing but the suppression of the old Adam or the natural man in us can fit us to use them aright. Why does Rousseau believe otherwise? For in some way he must now argue that the right use of art and science is natural to us, but that the abuse of them has somehow crept upon us in

[1] *Contrat social,* iii. 315.

defiance of our very nature. It would seem a desperate thesis,. but a good part of his thinking so far falls unless he can maintain it. So he must do this too while giving us the test for right and wrong.

His test has been forecast as far back as our instance of the tree, and several times since. As he believes our primal nature to be right, he must believe that all the art created in its image is right also, but that any other art is wrong. All art is right which simply enlarges us, but none is right if it distorts us. The good art is the rational development of our primal affections. But is this any more than reasoning in a circle? The right art is a growth out of our first affections; so of course our first affections are at peace with the right art. For answer let us look at what it all means in the light of our discoveries about those first affections. It means that if only reason will keep self-love true to our real needs, however these may grow with culture, and protect it from the lure of all imaginary needs, if only she will train our native sympathy into the rational benevolence which is its proper destiny, if only she will leave our conscience uncorrupted as a mediator between right and wrong as she discerns them, all will be well with us ; we shall remain natural and good, and be ready to flower into virtue. But if reason does any other thing, we shall begin to be unnatural and bad; and reason is under temptation to do all sorts of other things, as we have seen, and does them daily.

Yet a moment ago we were saying that the thing called pride caused all our ills, and now we seem to be laying them at the feet of errant reason. Precisely so. For if we only watch the work of reason, we shall see that every time she goes astray she is but yielding to the thing we have called pride. When we lay our tongue to lies, it is because we are too proud to tell the truth. When we abuse it for flattery or derision, we are only giving in to pride. If we forge a letter, it is always to exalt ourselves or to debase another. If we urge the worse against the better cause, it is only to get the best of an opponent. We have no possible inducement to abuse an art except to get ahead of some one else. And that is what we have called pride; there is no other sin. Search as we may in the misdeeds of reason, and we shall find that every one of them proceeds from pride. So

we cannot impute them to our natural sentiment, for pride is
only a corruption of a natural sentiment. They are therefore
not in our nature, but intrusions on us. They intrude whenever reason slips from the control of natural sentiment and
goes careering off after the rainbow, for she then has naught
but pride to snatch at for support. It is the unholy alliance
of the two that causes all our ills. And we must divorce reason
from pride and wed her anew to nature if we would be good.
Or once more, we must give up pride. Then we may return
to nature.

Once we have done so, we may follow reason to the summit
of art and science. It is her privilege to make us natural men in
civil life. She has already done much of the work, but she has
also done a good deal to the contrary. And her office now is to
renounce all that is contrary, and then build upward in the
better spirit. She could have no harder duty. There is nothing
harder than to return to nature, but nothing else is right. It
would be hard enough if the return to nature meant only going
back, but above all it means pressing forward. The best natural
man among us now is the man who, out of all the centuries of
culture back of us, has inherited the most that was born of the
better spirit and the least that is contrary to it. But the best of
all natural men will be the one who has a similar privilege at the
close of all the centuries.

This may be called perfectibility. The return to nature is
about the furthest cry that can be known from the primitivism
which its apostle is so often thought to have espoused. It is perfectibility on its own basis, of course, but about as surely such
as Condorcet's or Godwin's; and there might be a nice question whether its basis is broader or narrower than theirs.
Theirs was laid in reason only, and Rousseau's in reason and in
something more; but in order to make room for something
more, he had to put some limit upon reason itself. And this he
did because he thought it was the only rational thing to do;
because he felt that reason loosed from all responsibility to
natural sentiment would lead anywhere but to perfection. Of
course it is usual for perfectibilitarians to make more prophecies than Rousseau offers us; but as he was no great historian,
he was still less of a prophet. He was more intent on finding

the itinerary than in wondering how far we might pursue it. And it is that itinerary that he has been tracing here. Impelled by our nature to seek the good, we are provided with our reason to find it; and thus prompted and guided, we toil up toward virtue, which will be our end if we can reach it. Nature is right, and her name at last may be virtue.

III

But to toil upward we have need of one more gift. We must have the liberty to choose our path. For though we grow in reason till we can discern a hundred paths, we are only the more hopeless unless we grow concurrently in freedom to select the right one. So the chief of all our needs is liberty. We can have no moral life unless we are free, for there can be no right or wrong where all is necessary. A while ago we put off the inquiry as to what sets us apart from other creatures, and we may now return for an answer. It is not our first two sentiments; they are shared by other creatures, whether or not in comparable measure. It is usually said to be our reason; for whether or not the animals may show a semblance of the faculty, our reasoning is so peculiar in degree and kind that we may call it all our own. Yet if liberty to choose our courses does not grow in equal pace with reason to discern them, all our reasoning is still a mockery. If our acts are all necessitated, they will differ from an animal's only in the ceremonial that surrounds them, only in the little game of hocus-pocus that we call reflective thinking. But it is obvious that we enjoy a liberty of choice which the brutes know not. An animal choosing between two paths may or may not show some gleam of reason and concurrent freedom, but a man deciding among a hundred principles has come into a freedom out of all relation with the animal's. The brutes seek pleasure and shun pain as we do, but deliberate option of a principle to gain the pleasure proper to us is our gift alone. We are not defining free-will at the moment, and we shall not call it simple spontaneity when we come to do so.[1] For the present it is enough to say that we differ from all other creatures by a freedom in precise propor-

---

[1] See *post*, pp. 132–3.

tion to our reason. It is all that gives a value to our reason, or a moral meaning. It is therefore the thing that sets us truly apart.

Of course it is a dangerous gift. We can have no liberty to do the right without an equal liberty to choose the wrong. If our nature had been perfect, we could have known no freedom from the start. But it is not perfect, it is free; free to seek its own perfection or its own corruption.

But freedom is no one invariable thing at every step upon our journey upward. It is obviously one thing for a savage and a very different thing for Socrates. Like all our other gifts, it grows and alters gradually with every step we take. Yet the three great forms it passes through are readily distinguishable.

We begin with simple independence, or the form of freedom a wild animal enjoys. In one sense it is far from total. We are hemmed into our little round by all the laws of nature, by a legion of inexorable facts such as that fire will burn, that stones are hard, that we must eat to live, and that we shall fall if we miss our footing. We are absolutely dependent on earth, air, and water, and there are a thousand things we may not do for one we may. But no one cares about all this, for it is not in our nature to fret over it or to feel our freedom scanted by it. So in another sense the freedom is complete. Wholly dependent on the laws of things, we are wholly independent of the law of man, for man has not yet made a law. There may indeed be other men around us and impinging on us, but in the conditions we can only take them as so many other natural facts with which to reckon, take them as any brute must take his fellows. For we are simply brutes as yet. We owe no man allegiance, we can know no duty. We are wholly irresponsible, and within our powers we may do as we please. But whatever the glamour of doing as we please (and Rousseau often felt it all too keenly), we are in a pitiable state. For brute freedom to do as we please is only bondage to our pleasure; and the extremes meet when the freedom of the savage to glut appetite turns out to be slavery to appetite.

We rise next into civil liberty. This begins as soon as any group of us engages in a conscious common aim. The moment we make an agreement, however slight and vague, such as is necessary to unite us for a purpose, we have lost some portion of our utter independence. In due time we shall lose all the rest of it; for as soon as our society comes to be sovereign, as in reason and in practice it must do, we shall be free to do nothing except what it countenances, nothing merely because we so please. So our independence will vanish, not in part but wholly; and in its place will come civil liberty, or liberty properly so called. Independence was dependence on the laws of things alone; liberty involves dependence on the law of man as well. Independence knew no duty; liberty requires every act to be a duty. Independence knew no rights, for there could be no right when all did as they would, nor any power to fix one; in liberty our rights are fixed, and all the power of the group is engaged for their security. It is that security in rights that constitutes the liberty. What we have lost is therefore the precarious freedom to do as we please, and what we have gained is the assured freedom to do what all consider right.

And our state is the more gracious, provided always that no usurper comes to take away our rights again by force, and, far from giving back our former independence, merely wipes out every kind of freedom under tyranny. Such a disaster may make our society even worse than no society. But the good society, as we shall duly find, will know no tyranny, for it will fix as rights and duties all the things that reason finds appropriate to our nature. Whatever reason finds to have been natural for us in the old state of independence she will try to secure for us in the new condition of liberty, and so fulfil our nature; only we must remember that it is reason which is doing this, and that the rational way of satisfying a need in a society may be very different from the instinctive way of doing so before there was one—even as different as duty from desire. If we can but remember this, we shall learn that to fulfil our nature is always to be at liberty, and that if reason seeks no other end but such fulfilment, she must always leave us 'as free as hitherto';[1] and we shall be ready to begin the *Social Contract*.

Perfect obedience to our civil duty will bring us finally to know that highest form of freedom which is moral liberty. For in order to discharge our perfect duty to our fellows we must

[1] *Contrat social*, iii. 313.

master all our personal desires until our one desire is the good of all, or simple justice; until our desire is one with reason. Full submission to the law of reason means entire mastery of self, and the kingship over self is the final freedom. To will only the right is to be whole, an integer again, and free; to will the wrong is to put self at strife with reason, and whoso is at strife is not at liberty. To obey the law against our will is to be its slave, but to make our will one with the law is to be king. So when our will becomes autonomously one with principle we shall know the ultimate freedom. A high ideal certainly, and one which Kant may have borrowed here for fuller development; an ideal which may never be achieved, but which the few great souls of earth have striven for. A difficult ideal, for it is the one that has been before us all the way; to surrender self to principle is once more to give up pride.

And finally, to come into such virtue is to rise to happiness. The slave of desire will seek only satisfaction, and he cannot find that even, for desire will be led away by pride into the insatiable. But the master of desire may satisfy all the wants that he allows himself as right, and also attain the moral happiness that comes from wanting nothing more. He who could satisfy all possible desire would be content, but no one can do it; he who limits his desire to right reason will be blest. Virtue is its own reward because it is the only happiness, and pride is its own punishment because it makes every man a Tantalus. So the extremes meet again for the sage, who will be a Stoic with an Epicurean's guerdon—like many another Stoic. What indeed if he has been stoical to that end only? Was not Stoicism announced to us as the rugged road to happiness? But if he is stoical, he is not ascetic; he does not limit his desire to the minimum conceivable, for there is nothing natural in that, but only to exact equivalence with the true needs of his nature, or with right reason; for reason is right when she knows our true needs. And it was the father of all Stoics who said that 'The end of man is to live according to nature, which is to live according to virtue; for nature leads us into virtue.'[1]

Marginal notes: "Kant will deny This."; "Eudaemonia"; "Right Reason: fulfilling the needs posed by one's nature"

[1] Zeno *apud* Diogenes Laertius, ed. Cobet, 1850, p. 178: διόπερ πρῶτος ὁ Ζήνων ἐν τῷ περὶ ἀνθρώπου φύσεως τέλος εἶπε τὸ ὁμολογουμένως τῇ φύσει ζῆν, ὅπερ ἐστὶ κατ' ἀρετὴν ζῆν· ἄγει γὰρ πρὸς ταύτην ἡμᾶς ἡ φύσις.

IV

What we have now put together is not to be found intact at any given place in Rousseau's work. All the main ideas are patent there in passages of greater length and of the utmost clarity; they are frequently repeated, and could hardly be put forward more insistently; and when they are assembled, they leave few interstices and fairly little option for the joiner's art. So even if we have made more errors than are pardonable in piecing them together, we may hope that in the main we have shown fairly what our author meant to say.

It is quite true that there are passages from him, most of them written when his thought was struggling into birth, which seem to contradict our meaning. Far too much has been made of them. As we go on, we shall find that most of them will harmonize with what we have been saying if we will but make sure of their intention instead of tripping over their terms. Perhaps some of them will remain irreconcilable. But so much was expected at the start. Rousseau was not a man to leave all trim; he was a man to make the most of the idea immediately before him rather than to shape it into careful consonance with all the other ideas in his mind. And while he is not utterly unique in this, we have shown that he is capable upon occasion of throwing off a phrase which can all too easily be wrested from the main intention of his work and even urged against it. We all know he once said that 'the man who meditates is a degenerate animal'. If that is what he meant, if that is all he meant, then all that we have said about him so far must be false; all that we have found him saying about reason and virtue and liberty must somehow be abominable to him, and we can only be left marvelling why he took such pains to court obloquy by saying it. But which did Rousseau mean, that wretched sentence or the *Social Contract* and *Emile*? It may seem childish to ask such a question, but it is necessary because far more than half the world has thought he meant the first. If the summary here given is wrong, it can hardly be amended by citing an egregious paradox or two against it from our author. It can be replaced, and should be, only by a truer summary which will show what the author of *Emile* was trying to do.

There is little purpose to appraise the doctrine here. All the criticism we have given of it is meant only to keep it clear of misinterpretation. We are quite aware that our summary does not make a perfect unity, and that parts of it may easily be cited against other parts; we are not trying to smooth over any part, but only to report our author's utterance at every point. If we can get his meaning clear, we would rather leave the question of its truth or value to the reader. But all experience warns us that we ought to put the reader on his guard. If he sees no reason for the fact as yet, his state is possibly the more gracious, for he has never set his foot in the Serbonian bog of Rousseau criticism. If ever he in turn should read a thousand or more books and articles about Rousseau in the effort to make sure of the meaning, he will know but too well how hard it is to keep his head. But whether he comes finally to think that Rousseau is mainly right or mainly wrong—and we may intrude a moment to say that we have never felt wise enough to be sure—we may hope he will conclude that it is high time to cease from talking of our author in the tone of some of the quotations with which we started and with which we could go on in tens of thousands.

For it is time to stop saying that Rousseau never learned to think if we would ever learn to think about him. It is time to stop repeating that his work is nothing but a matchless gallimaufry of phantasms or a poison secreted from a soul rotted with sentimentalism. It is time to quit declaring that he wrote 'more nonsense, far more, than all the other great classics put together'.[1] It is time to cease from thinking of him only as a sort of Original Sin from whom nearly all the sins of thought or flesh since him have sprung. It is time to know that we are not done with his doctrine when we have called him a 'hoot-owl', a 'charlatan savage', an 'enemy of the human race', a 'hypocrite', a 'traitor', a 'blackguard', a 'hyena', a 'Swiss valet', a 'valet of Diogenes', or, sinking ever lower in the biological scale, a 'bastard of the dog of Diogenes and the bitch of Herostratus'. If we pause, it is for shame and not for

[1] Lemaître, *Jean-Jacques Rousseau*, p. 248.

lack of epithets; there are exactly thirty-three more in Voltaire alone, from whom all these have come.[1] And let no one imagine that the critics of our own day, if less lively, are less bitter or fantastic. As you read *Emile*, queries Lasserre, do you not smell 'the odour of a corpse'[2]? And something similar will be found on every page of Lasserre, and on almost every page of Lemaître, Seillière, Nourrisson, Espinas, and many more in many languages. The criticism of Rousseau has gone beyond anything that he himself predicted of the arts and sciences in the callow essay on them which brought his name before the world and of which he was afterwards ashamed. So the reader will see why we have put him on his guard.

The idea that man must be perfected by his reason in accordance with his nature runs through all of Rousseau's work and gives it an essential unity. The *Discourse on the Sciences and Arts* is a sally at the corruption that science and art have brought upon us, and it is so injudicious that it often reads as if they had brought us nothing else. Its author leaped into immediate fame for his belief that the natural man is good; so in the *Discourse on Inequality* he has to say exactly what he means by a natural man and to recount the history of man from the earliest times to ours. And the natural man turns out to be no mere primeval brute, but a man of our own day or rather of a future day; so *Emile* is the attempt to make one man what all men should be in the future. But the ideal man can live only in an ideal society, and the *Social Contract* therefore seeks to build a perfect state out of the very nature of the men composing it. During our brief stay in it, our most important question is about our destiny beyond all the states of this world; and that is the question in the *Savoyard Vicar's Profession of Faith*, which is meant to be the natural religion—the religion, that is, to which we all may come if we listen only to our sentiment and reason.

Education, government, religion, these are the three great matters for whoso would bring man to the perfection of his nature. They are anything but separate, save for the convenience of our thinking; so nearly all the *Social Contract* will be

---

[1] See the full list in Vallette, *Jean-Jacques Rousseau genevois*, p. 396, n. 2.
[2] *Le Romantisme français*, p. 70.

found within *Emile*, and everything in *Emile* lies behind the *Social Contract*; while the Savoyard Vicar is a character in *Emile* itself, and his essential articles of faith are made into the state religion of the *Contract*. And of course Rousseau is treating the same subjects nearly everywhere else. The *New Héloïse* is full of doctrine on them all. The *Letters from the Mount*, much longer than the *Savoyard Vicar*, form only one of several treatises making up the body of religious thought in which the Vicar's *Profession* is the soul. The two volumes of *Political Writings*, as now collected,[1] comprise a considerable cluster of essays around the brief *Contract*. Even the *Confessions* and the other autobiographical work done under partial taint of madness in old age exhibit, among other purposes, the desire to tell as much as possible about one man for whatever it may prove about our nature. So these and all the other works will be before us as we now look for what our doctrine comes to in the realms of education, government, religion.

[1] Ed. C. E. Vaughan, 1915.

II

THE NATURAL EDUCATION

TO return to nature, then, is by no means to go back to
savagery. It is as necessary for us to rise out of savagery
into culture as out of infancy into manhood, and we may continue natural at every point in the ascent, though only by
being somewhat different from what we are at any other point;
by being not immutable, but evermore adaptable. One way to
be unnatural, were it possible, is to decline the ascent or to
turn back once we have begun it. Another way, only too
possible, is to stray out of the right path we have found for it
into any of the tempting mazes deviating from it. To be
natural is just to keep from getting lost; and to keep us from
getting lost is the office of education.

So the next thing in Rousseau is *Emile*—the story of a boy
who must never once stray out of the right path from infancy
to manhood. The boy will become the natural man of our day;
and we have seen that such a man is one who inherits all the
culture of the past that is accordant with his primal principle and
escapes all that is at variance with it. But if the idea is easy to
phrase, it is hard enough to carry out, and we may be ready for
some errors in its main initiator.

'I demurred a long while over publishing the book . . . but after vain
efforts to make it better, I believe I ought to print it as it is . . and though
my own notions may be erroneous, I shall not have lost my time if I inspire better ones in others . . . I may be wrong about the means to use, but
I think I am right about the end to aim for.'[1]

If the aim to form a natural man was not altogether new,
the general problem of an education was about as old as any;
and though Rousseau is original enough to be properly called
revolutionary, he is so familiar with his predecessors as to offer
hardly an idea that he had not read in one or more of them. In
a general way he goes as far back as the *Republic*, which he calls
the greatest of all books on education. In detail he owes more

[1] ii. 1, 2.

to Montaigne, and apparently, though not so certainly, to
Rabelais. He read all the Port-Royal treatises, and absorbed
the 'sainted Fénelon', the 'good Rollin', and the 'learned
Fleury'. Above all he pondered the 'wise Locke', master of all
the educational thinking in the period, and incurred a debt so
large that he occasionally tried to disguise it, none too grate-
fully, by making the most of the very real divergencies between
them. Nearer his own time he knew a dozen or more treatises
of less importance, issuing mainly out of Locke; for many of
the men around him saw in education the prime means to their
great end of making the world over. He encountered a good deal
of educational theory in editing the work of the Abbé de Saint-
Pierre. His friend Grimm planned an extensive treatise on the
subject, and Helvetius actually wrote one. His patroness
Madame d'Épinay wrote two, one prior to his own; and a little
earlier Madame de Graffigny had entered the field.[1] It was to
her that Turgot had addressed the little disquisition which,
though Rousseau seems never to have known of it, comes
nearest to his own in its insistence upon nature as the single
test of all our educational art. 'Nature has put into the heart of
man the seeds of every virtue; we have but to let them grow.'[2]
The words of Turgot promise all of *Emile*, with only the large
difference between bud and flower. But we have seen that the
idea was already old; and when we call Rousseau its main
initiator, we can only mean that he gave it far ampler meaning
than it had ever known before. That is what made a revolution.

The one question that matters here is whether that idea is
right or wrong. Did nature start us on the right way and leave
education the one office of helping us along it, or did she put us
on the wrong road and provide our education with the task of
rescuing us from it? If the first, our book may well be wrong in
many a particular, but will be right in principle and open to
correction in detail; if the second, it is wrong at bottom, and
pernicious; it can stumble on occasional truth only by straying
from its very principle. And the problem is still real for us,
whether we put it in the terms of Rousseau or in those we think

---

[1] Mme. d'Épinay, *Lettres à mon fils*, 1758, and *Les Conversations d'Émilie*, 1783;
Mme. de Graffigny, *Lettres d'une péruvienne*, 1747.
[2] *Œuvres*, 1844, ii. 793.

more modern. We shall find ourselves returning to it as the crucial question after we have heard what Rousseau has to say.

But if we would hear him in the hope of being ready for the question when it comes, we must first get rid of certain issues that should never have obscured it. The answer to them may be obvious, but it seems necessary. For not only are they the first objections that occur to any reader of the book, but they comprise a good three-quarters of the printed criticism of it.

It is objected that our author cannot carry out his own design. To keep a boy in the path at every moment, he would have to follow every moment of the boy's life, and his book would never end. The answer is that he does not pretend to register the boy's every thought and act. He lays down the leading principles, with occasional illustration, and must leave the tutor to apply them to the passing moment. And of course the tutor too will lack the time and vigilance to make sure of every instant; but the best tutor, other things equal, is the one who comes the nearest to so doing.

It is objected that the author has no faith in his design. Did he not lay down one discipline for Emile and another for the boys in Poland? For example, did he not keep his own boy ignorant of history into adolescence and then make the little Poles learn all their patriotic record at a tender age? In fact, did he not tell a certain M. Anga (a consequential fellow, possibly, but let that pass) that he was a fool for bringing up his son according to *Emile*? And what does that mean but lack of faith in his own book? Yet no man ever wrote an *Emile* without believing in it. And the answer is that Emile is meant to be the natural man of any place or station in a civil world and thus to have the education that should be common to all men within the civil order. Of course he ought to have as much more as may be compatible with this and necessary for his individual place and station; and according as he is a Frenchman or a Pole or Japanese, according as he may become a pewterer or a prince, he will need a good deal more, and of an infinite variety. But all that is peculiar to a given man and needless or impossible to another is beyond our author's scope, or again his book would have no end. He may well allow for such things if he ever comes to teach the boys of any given land from Poland to Peru, and he may find some adaptation of his principles advisable. For the present he is thinking of the education every man should have; and every man should be an Emile, though each one should be as much else, in addition and by way of adaptation, as his place and calling may require.

It is objected that the plan is a chimera. In his earlier years the boy is taken out of almost all society except his tutor's, and not only is it evil to deprive him of the education he would get from playmates, but it is impossible to find a vacant spot inhabitable for the pair. And though the boy may be an average child, the tutor is a paragon beyond discovery. Among other things, he will give his every thought to the one boy, will remain unmarried, take no wages, and never train a second pupil; and the world will soon come to starvation and depopulation. It would be easier to omit these criticisms if they had not been advanced so often and so gravely as affairs that somehow never dawned upon our author. Yet he knew that children learn a great deal from their playmates and that there are not sufficient vacant places to sequester a few hundred millions of them with their tutors. These and all the other facts he would consider if he ever set up school in Poland or elsewhere. But to find the aim for all schools he will first place the boy of his fancy in ideal conditions and see what the ideal man resulting may mean for the men of every day. And the answer to all these objections is that *Emile* is a counsel of perfection. 'I propose the end to aim for; I do not say that we can reach it, but I hold that he who comes the nearest to it is the most successful.'[1] It will never be achieved in practice, but it may endure as the ideal of all practice. By that token it may be more truly practical than any other plan. A plan that we can realize to-day may well be antiquated by the morrow, but the ideal we can never realize may be potent for all time. No Republic has been known as yet, but the one in Plato goes on shaping states of which the last is out of all imagination. And no Emile has yet been seen, but no other figure has had such an influence in the school-rooms of the world. So the only ques-

[1] ii. 62.

tion is whether that influence is for good or evil. That was our first query, and must be our last.

It may be gathered that we are not going to be very busy over the specific subjects we must teach our boy. Whether he shall learn a little Latin, for example, or a great deal, will depend upon his place and station. There were good men before there was a Latin language, and there are many now who have no need of it; according to the place and station it may be essential or unnecessary or ridiculous, while many other things may be far more important. And in all our mental discipline the aim will be to find the way of teaching any subject rather than to argue for a given one, or to fit our boy's mind for learning any rather than to cram it with the few that are traditional. But the mental training, though so commonly the whole of education, will not be the major part in ours. The training of the body will be almost as important as that of the mind, and the moral discipline will outweigh both. For we are aiming at an ideal man, or the man we have been calling natural, and such is the relative importance of the elements that go to form him. But the man we seek will have them all in harmony.

For a first principle we may say that there are three kinds of education. There is an education in just growing up—in the development of our faculties and organs that simply comes of its own motion. Then there is the education we receive from all the things around us in the world—from the facts that stones are hard and heavy, that fire is hot and hills are steep, and from a myriad other things of great importance, all unknown to us at first and all learned without any need of teaching. And finally there is the education we receive from men. The first kind of education is entirely out of our control, the second mainly so, and the third alone wholly within it. So the first of all our principles must be that the one in our control must keep peace with the two that are beyond it. Otherwise we shall be flying in the face of changeless fact. And this means that we must teach our boy any given thing only when the growth of his own faculties has brought him to the point where he can master it. If the statement seems a truism, we may find out more about it later.

In the growth of our faculties we go through four main

periods. These are not divided by precise lines, and of course we drift unconsciously from one into another; nor are they the same exactly for all individuals. But in rough division we may say that the first period will run until the age of four or five, the second until twelve or thirteen, the third until about sixteen, and the fourth up to maturity. The four are seen as fairly real divisions in the four books of the treatise we devote to them.

I

In the period of infancy there can be but little positive instruction. By that token there must be the utmost care to keep the infant from forsaking nature, or from being led away from her, before he knows what is occurring. So our author will begin with the first hour, and from the moment when he leaves the wine out of the baby's bath he will hold to the one aim of keeping him in nature's way.

Hence the celebrated diatribe against the system of detaching babies from their mothers and of quartering them with nurses in the country; and in particular against the use of the *maillot* in which the baby was encased to keep him out of harm's way or the nurse's, and in which he might be even hung up on the wall for the greater comfort of his elders. What Rousseau had to say about the practice is too well known for repetition, and indeed it had been said so many times before him that a man like Buffon was but human in complaining when the mothers would not listen until Rousseau joined the cry. But it may be noted that Rousseau is less angry at the physical discomfort of the *maillot* than at the moral lesson it conveyed in earliest infancy—less because it weakened lung and limb, and doubtless had its part in the death of every other child in France before the age of eight, than because it brought a sense of slavery with the first milk and engendered a dumb hatred of the very persons meant to foster love; because it took the infant out of nature at the very start.

In its stead Rousseau would leave him free to range and pull and haul to his content. It is a poor parent who cannot see that dangerous or valuable things are put beyond his reach, and an unthinking one who fancies that a child has any instinct to destroy. The child is all activity, of course, and since he cannot know enough to put a thing together he will certainly take it apart. Even in so doing he is slowly learning a good deal, and we may leave him free to test and shift and try experiment upon the world that is so new to him. He will find out a little host of things about it that will constitute his earliest education, none the less important though it comes upon him unaware. Thus a world that started as a big blur for him gradually takes on certain shapes and properties inviting him to see what he can do with them for his own purposes. And therein is about all the positive education he can have as yet. It is mainly out of our control. We may help a little by laying out the world around him so as to allow the best experiments in the best conditions, but otherwise we must leave him pretty much alone to find out the first few thousand facts that he will know.

We are no less busy for all that, and we shall need the utmost care and wisdom if we are to keep our mite of nature in the way that nature plans for him. It is her way to make the child so weak as not to be sufficient for himself, and us so strong that we can satisfy his needs as well as our own. And it is therefore natural that he should feel his weakness and our strength, and should be conscious of his own dependence on us. But there is grave danger that his weakness or our strength or both will be abused beyond the purposes of nature.

There is danger that we may be so harassed by him as to scold or spank him to submission. The gravity of such an act will dawn upon us if we only think of what it has to mean to him. He can have no way of knowing we are doing it for his own good, if so we are, nor can we find a way of telling him; and all that we can possibly arouse in him will be a feeling that we are using our superior power to deny his wish and give him pain. If he cannot phrase this as we do, he will feel it none the less acutely. So one of the first lessons that we give him will be that of servitude—a very different thing from the dependence we were calling natural. We have a little slave in the making.

Or we may be so distressed about his cries as to indulge and coddle him till he is 'spoiled'. He will learn that he need only cry to set us bustling with cajolery; and he will soon be crying ever and anon from no true need, but solely for the love of spoiling. That alone is bad enough; but it is still worse that out of his very weakness he has learned, instead of natural dependence, a spirit to command and dominate. We now have a little tyrant in the making.

And very often we have slave and tyrant both by fits and starts. Thus slavery and tyranny are the two highways out of nature that we are prone to put before an infant, the two paths into the boundless realm of what we have called pride. We are in such danger of them both that nothing in our book is more ideal than the resolution to avoid them. We must be all wisdom to supply the true needs of our infant and to do no more or less.

We may put this in specific instance. We have just been speaking of the things our boy learns in rummaging around his little world. At the very first he must feel that he is all of it, for he can be aware of no distinction yet between himself and all the things around him. Even when he first begins to know they are outside him, he will see them all without perspective, all at equal distances from him, or at no distance. Only through some sort of motion will he learn that they are outside him, and only through his own motion will he find out that they are set apart from him by certain distances. All of this he learns in ranging, and beyond his reach we may assist by ranging for him—by bringing him an object that he cannot reach, or, better still, by taking him to it and giving him a chance to draw the natural inference in due time. Now when he first reaches out for things, he can have no notion that they are beyond him. We shall take him to them, and keep doing so till he has learned the salutary fact that there are things beyond his grasp. But once we have made sure he knows it, we must take him only when there is a reason. If he cries about it, we must let him utterly alone; there will be no other way to stop him from desiring to cry. He is either ordering a thing to come to him or us to bring it; and he must know that he is not to order men around, for he is not their master, and is not to give commands to things, for they will not listen. Once he has learned this, and only then, he will not want to cry.

We may now make the instance general. In his weakness he has no petition to us but a cry. At the first it cannot but express a true need, for he knows of no dissembling. We must satisfy it instantly if possible. But in time there is a danger of his conjuring up a little set of fancied needs, and we must be as careful to ignore these as to satisfy the true ones. We must not scold or punish him for them, for that will teach him slavery again, but we may be simply deaf to them until his nascent tyranny proves vain and dies of inanition. Such is the one way to end it, for repression only drives it into other channels, all of pride. If we merely pet or beat him till he ceases crying for the present, we shall find his pride and tears redoubled on the morrow. There is but one way to keep him natural.

For that purpose we may try the following general rules. 1. Let him use the little strength he has, in the assurance that he will find no way to abuse it. 2. Aid him by supplying all the strength he needs to satisfy his true wants. 3. Stop short with the true wants and ignore all whim and fantasy. 4. Use all care to make sure which are true and which are fanciful. 'The spirit of the rules is to allow more freedom and less domination, or to let the infant do more for himself and demand less of others.'[1]

II

Much of this will hold into the following period. As the boy advances from a life of mere sensation into one of nascent understanding which will bring us cares of greater number and complexity, we must still be true at least to our first principle of giving him the training that his years will justify. We are caring for a child, and our first duty is to let him be one.

Only for a moment longer will the statement seem a truism. We may say at once that Rousseau meant it for about the opposite of what the tutors of his day were doing. In his mind they were less eager to preserve a childhood for their children than to hoist them into manhood at all speed and any cost. And he knew the reason for it. He knew all the pressure put upon a tutor to transform a child into a little sage who would do precocious honour to the doting parents of an artificial world. He could but deplore the fact that the fortune of the tutor thus depended on the speed with which he could contrary nature by coaxing or scolding his little charge into a semblance of maturity before the season due. The aim was wrong, and

[1] ii. 37.

really hopeless; it was all a little game of make-believe. For
we cannot bring the child to be a man till nature wills it. We
may fill him with the airs and phrases of a man, or teach him
how to cheat himself and others, but we can no more give him
the feeling and the understanding proper to such manners at the
age of six than we can make him six feet tall at that time, and we
should have a monster for a child if we could do so. We can
only rob him of his childhood in the vain endeavour to up-
heave him into manhood, and the worst of that is that we
weaken or destroy the only basis on which the right sort of
manhood can be built. We sacrifice the present to the future,
and must sacrifice the future in its turn. If we would have our
boy natural, we must leave him free to be a child.

But we must have him anything except a chartered libertine,
nor is it any plan of nature that he be one. By her order we
must govern him because he is too weak to use the kind of
freedom we enjoy. By her further order we must give him any
kind of freedom he can use if we would ever make him strong.
And so far we have been trying to obey her two commands.
For in his infancy we have been fairly Spartan with our discipline, though only in the aim of giving him the fuller freedom.
In the anxious period now beginning we must find a way to
rule with equal rigour but allow an equal liberty. We must try
to leave him free and keep him in control at once. And the
way to do the two things will require some discussion. It may
show the kind of freedom proper to a child.

Man has a place within the natural order, and the child a
place within the human order; and possibly the truth that we
have found about the one may help us to a truth about the
other. We have found that there is only one thing which will
lure us from content in nature's order. It is pride. It will take
us out of nature into discontent and slavery because it is insatiable; and we cannot be free or happy if we are for ever longing
for the things we cannot have. We are free and happy just as
long as we can limit our desire to our strength—just as long as
we attend to our true needs, or cleave to nature and avoid pride.

Then what do we mean in saying that the child is weak while
we are strong? No creature can be weak whose forces equal
his desires, nor any strong when his desire has outrun his

force. The tiniest one is strong enough if he may have his every wish, and the mightiest too weak if he must fail of any. So when we say that we are feeble creatures we can only mean that we have given in to pride and are unable to keep pace with it; for, like every other creature, we are equal to our true needs. And when we say that a child is weak while we are strong, we cannot mean merely that he has less force of mind and body than ourselves, for there are many able creatures with far less than his, but rather that he is as yet unequal to his true needs, and would perish in a day or two without our aid.

So the child's place in the human order is one of dependence. It is very natural that he should feel it, and very necessary that it should be absolute if we would keep him in the proper place at every moment. Any sort of freedom fit for him must be at peace with these necessities. It cannot be the lowest form of freedom which will let him do as he may please, for that would be fatal to him. It cannot be one of the higher forms that we have mentioned, for they are utterly beyond him; they are open to the sage who knows his place in nature and has the wisdom to abide in it. The child knows nothing of his natural place, and we alone can keep him to it. Is there any sort of freedom left for him—any art to keep him under absolute control and yet allow him to feel free?

We have said that there are two kinds of dependence. One is an invariable dependence on the things around us—on time and tide, on heat and cold, on all the natural law which no one may evade. Just because we cannot dodge it in the smallest point we remain untroubled by it, and our full submission leaves us feeling free. No one but a lunatic will ever fret because he cannot live in fire or leap over the moon. The other is a variable dependence upon man, and often open to evasion. And in part because we can evade it on occasion, we are often tempted to the effort. For it is in our nature not to care about the stringent limits of the natural law but to resent the interference of an alien will.

The child is under both sorts of dependence. Subject to the things around him, he must furthermore be subject to our own control if he is to endure. But he can have no way of really knowing this. He will never understand as we do that our control of him is for his higher good or future happiness, how-. ever often we repeat the phrases to him. Still less will he gather what we mean by right and wrong, or duty, if we use the words with him. If he knew their meaning at the end of infancy he would hardly need a further education. In his ignorance he can but feel, as we shall see if we will take his place a moment, that all our control is simple interference from an alien will. So he will resent it and evade it if he can, and hamper all our efforts for his good. That at least is what will happen unless we find a way to wield it that will leave him feeling free.

There can be but one way. We may let our will control him in the simple manner of the things around him; then he will not dream of fretting at it or of feeling the less free for it. If we flourish our authority upon him, he will fail to understand it and be driven to resent it; if we simply let it rest on him like any natural law, he will offer no resistance and will feel at liberty. He will feel dependent on us, as he should, but just as he will feel dependent on the earth and air. In so far as we can wield a will as calm, impartial, and irrevocable as a law of nature, we shall have the child in full control and yet in freedom. And if this appear a counsel of perfection, any other is of imperfection.

Thus the child will do our will without obeying us. Obedience means a knowledge of his duty that is still beyond him. In its absence, he will do as he must until he shall be capable of doing as he ought. He will ask of us without commanding, for he has already found a whining order useless. We shall not prohibit him from wrong, for he will not understand the word, but simply keep him clear of it. We shall avoid all excess of rigour that would make him wretched now as well as all indulgence that would make him suffer later. But in all things we shall govern him by simple force—not the fitful and capricious force that seems punition, but a steady and beneficent one that no more hints of punishment than does any other law of nature.

In a word, we shall not reason with a little child. Nature will arrange for him to reason later. She will keep his reason for the latest of her gifts, or for a sort of product of the rest. We may hardly use it to produce the rest, and must rely on other means.[1] If we call on reason to deny his wish at present, we are only helping him to hate her before he can know her; and if we mingle any of the ordinary threats or punishments in the appeal, we are making her more unattractive still. Even if we train the boy to glibness in the terms of reason long before he knows their meaning, we are once more fostering the vice of cheating with words (*se payer de mots*), or of thinking that he knows a thing when he knows nothing but its name. Instead of this we shall employ the power that controls without constraining, and keep reason for a more attractive presentation. We shall use reason with a man, but force with our child. It is the natural way.

If so natural, why has it required so much art to find? We have said that it very often takes the highest art to find the natural way of action in an artificial world, but that there is still no opposition between nature and the right art. Far back in the 'state of nature' parents doubtless did about as we have been advising. They employed simple force with their offspring, and it was accepted as a natural fact that did not seem to lessen liberty. They could make no more appeal to reason or authority than other brutes could, or than earth and air can. Their problem was exceeding simple, and their instinct was enough to solve it. Our own problem takes as much more art as it is more complex. And if the right art turns out to be similar to the way of ancient instinct, with allowance for all differences involved, it is right not by that token, but because it holds in reason. We need hardly be surprised to find our art prolonging and perfecting nature.

'Treat your child according to his age. Put him in his natural place from the beginning and hold him there so firmly that he will never dream of quitting it. Long before he knows what wisdom is, he will then be living by its most important law. Never give him a command of any kind; never let him fancy that you claim authority to do so. Simply let him know that he is weak and you are strong, and that in the nature of the case he lives in your control. Let him learn at once the full force of the law that nature puts upon his lordly head, the stern law of necessity to which all finite creatures have to bow; but let him learn it as necessity, and not as

---

[1] A little later Rousseau will be speaking of a *kind* of reason granted to a child and open to great cultivation. It may be well to say this here, while leaving all distinctions to a later page.

your caprice. Keep him out of wrong without an act of prohibition, and without debate or disquisition. Grant him all he ought to have at his first word, and never wait for him to beg or importune you; above all, never stop to make conditions. Grant always with pleasure, and refuse only with reluctance, but let a refusal be so irrevocable as to leave him no temptation to exhaust his forces in the hope to break it down. So you shall keep him patient, calm, and happy.[1]

And you will have done the two things that appeared in-consonant—kept him under full control and left him free. Such the freedom proper to a child, and such the right control. If it will be better than appeals to reason, it will be still better than the use of emulation, vanity, or fear as motives; for what sort of plan is it to plant a vice with every lesson? 'Liberty well governed' is the best plan, though it may well be the hardest.

Such is the idea of a 'negative education', to use at last the famous phrase which has been misconstrued almost as often as it has been approved or reprobated. It does not mean that our boy will be idle, for he will find his time full with the positive education proper to him. But it does mean that he will care-fully be kept in ignorance of certain things which other boys of his age are commonly required to know but which we believe improper for him till he can more fully understand them. Not to understand is to misunderstand; and not only is ignorance better than error, but a misconception once begun will dis-appear with difficulty, if at all. The first truism for our author was to teach what could be understood, and he is now to show that he meant more than may have been expected. Of course he draws up no one catalogue of things unteachable to children, and would look upon the following list as more illustrative than final; but he offers it in ample instance of his principle.

The child is shielded from all study of mere symbols. In his eye a symbol is too likely to become the thing it stands for, and he ought to see the thing itself. 'What is the world? It is a globe made out of carton.' Rousseau seems to remember a geography that opened with the words; and he is sure it is the kind of lesson many a boy learns from maps and spheres. The boy had better start geography upon the ground in front of him. Two years later he may be less ready with a list of towns

[1] ii. 58.

and countries like Pekin and Mexico that have so little meaning
for him except on the map, but he may have the rather rare
ability to sketch a road from Paris to Saint-Denis, and his
knowledge will be real as a foundation for the rest to
come.

He is shielded from all history. He could learn the names
of kings and emperors, of course, of wars and revolutions; but
his mind would stop short with the names, or just beyond
them. History is the tale of all the highest agonies and victories
of men, and no one but a man can have the passion and the
understanding to know what it means. What will Alcibiades
or Marius mean to a child when there are so many mysteries in
his own father and mother? He will suffer nothing from his
ignorance of the names till he can understand the men, and then
he can soon learn the names.

He is shielded from all fables, even La Fontaine's. Rousseau
might have left this out as trifling if he had not been so prone
to make the most of minor heresies, and if indeed he had considered anything a trifle for the boy whom he is keeping in the
right way every moment. At any rate, he means it in all earnest.
And just because it seems a trifle upon which he is so like himself in carrying out his principle to the last extreme, it may offer
the best occasion to refer a reader to the full discussion in the
book as a good place to test the principle at its weakest. If the
reader finds it wrong, he may then inquire whether anything
left of the principle is right; but he ought to be sure that he can
show it wrong first. The subtle fox flatters the stupid crow
upon his vocal powers until the crow lifts up his voice to
raucous song and drops his bit of cheese down to the fox, who
gulps it with a flash of cynicism about trusting flatterers. Every
child of six in France can say the pretty verses. What does he
make of them? Is it well for him to know that there are men
who live by flattery and fraud? Whom will he admire, the
cheat of a fox or the poor honest crow? Which will he try to
be? In all honesty, has he learned more about guarding himself
from flattery or about seducing others by it? If the questions
sound a bit Johnsonian in the premises, they may be Johnsonian also in the fact that they cannot be answered by a shriek,
but only by a reason. Possibly the reason can be found, but

Rousseau did not see it when he held that fables are for men, and a more literal truth for children.

The child is shielded from abstract ideas. In supreme example, he will hear of no abstractions about right and wrong. These are hard enough for any of us, and what sage indeed has shown us just what right and wrong are? We have nothing more important than to keep the child from wrong and in the right, but we have found out that the proper way is to habituate him to the right long before we try to set him reasoning about it. Give him the names for things he cannot know, and he is bound to put a meaning on them more or less erroneous or grotesque—a meaning that will often pass our own imagination to foresee. At the least this brings the vice of cheating with his words, and at the most it plants monstrosities that may never be uprooted and will always leave their traces even if they are.

That is why the child is shielded from the most important thing of all. He will never hear the name of God till he is nearly grown. Not that it will then be in his power, though he prove a sage indeed, to fathom all the mystery; but at least he may escape the strange and unintentionally sacrilegious notions that must fill him if he is forced to think about it now. Children hear of God about the age of four. What can they imagine but a very big man, almost as great as their own father? And in vain, to Rousseau, all our other explanations. We may say that God is spirit, and whatever we may mean in our own mind, the child will probably think of something like a ghost, and of a ghost as something like a mist in moonlight. We may ask ourselves if we are free of sacrilege in fostering such an image in him. Will he ever quite get over it? How many of us have done so? How often do we think of heaven without the pearl and gold that we now know would be the vilest trumpery to us there?

But even children must believe in God to be saved? The duty to believe presumes the power; there is no way to believe a thing if we cannot conceive it. If a child can think of nothing but a big man, or a ghost or moonlit mist, he can certainly believe no more. And if we are going to teach him of a God who will damn a child for not confusing him with moonlit mist, we had better not breathe our religion to the child. Nothing he can conjure up will be so hideous. So we shall not talk of these things with him. We shall wait till he is fitted for a reverence at least equal to our own; and in its insufficiency we shall then summon all of it for the supreme lesson we shall have to give him.

Such the things from which our author would protect his boy. But where is he to hide the prodigy of innocence from other men and boys who will talk of them? He knows well enough he cannot hide him. He knows the boy will hear too much and ask for more—in questions that will puzzle any one to answer in a manner to allay and not to stimulate improper curiosity. Our author has not announced the negative education as a facile one, but as the right one—as a thing beyond achievement which alone is worth our trying to achieve. It is what he would accomplish if he could, and what he will approach as nearly as he can. 'I see the difficulties, and we may not overcome them all; but I am sure that if we do our best we shall surmount a certain number of them.[1]' And there is difference enough between doing all we can to put off the improper things and doing all we can to speed their coming. We may put them off as long as possible, and may impart them when we must in the most practical example rather than in any abstract principle.

But once the boy is out of innocence he is liable to vice, and we must begin thinking of correction and punition. Of course our author hates all punishment as such, and yet would have it so severe as to make the boy loathe a wrong that he has done. To that end the punishment must come as no expression of the tutor's grief or anger at a deed, but as the simple product of the deed itself reacting on the doer. The easy way is to declaim against the fault and whip the boy; the hard and wise one is to let the fault recoil on him in such discomfort as will make it unalluring to repeat. Then he will loathe the vice itself instead of loathing the tutor—will loathe it even though he may be able to hide it from the tutor. But it is so much better to forestall a vice than to uproot it that Rousseau has far more to say of cause and of prevention than of cure. He will take the vice of lying as illustrative.

[1] ii. 62.

What can make a boy lie to us? He may do it to deny a deed that is displeasing to us or to promise one that will be pleasing without meaning to perform it. In either case his motive is to shun our anger. But if we have brought him up by the preceding principles, we have never let the motive dawn upon him. We have been no alien will opposing him and dealing out our pleasure and displeasure in rewards and punishments. We have been like a natural force controlling him without diminishing his sense of freedom and without even trying to explain our own beneficent necessity. We have never offered to command him, never told him that he must obey us. What could make him lie to us? He can have no interest but to tell the simple truth.

So a child is not the natural liar we so often call him. 'All the lies of a child are the work of a master.'[1] Only in demanding his obedience under pain of our own anger do we train him to deceive us. Only in allowing him no motive for deception may we keep him telling us the natural truth. And so with many other faults; just as any haste to train him to the principle of truth before he can know its meaning will lead him into lies, so will any hurry to prescribe the other duties drive him into the evasions which make up the other vices. We may better keep him to all duty without giving him the reason for it now. 'You mustn't do that,' says the master; and if we will only take the child's place for a moment we shall see what has to follow, unless he has already learned evasion:

'Why not?'
'Because it is wrong.'
'But what does that mean?'
'It means doing what you are forbidden.'
'What is the harm in that?'
'You will be punished for disobedience.'
'I shan't let anybody know.'
'You will be watched.'
'I shall hide.'
'You will be questioned.'
'I shall lie.'
'You mustn't lie!'

ii. 70.

'Why not?'

'Because it is wrong.'

And so on. How are we going to alter the dialogue? Rousseau sees no way to change it, and would therefore never start it. And he has now told us all that he would try to do instead.

Whether he is mainly right or wrong, he need not be mis-read as meaning that the child will never have to do unpleasant things for their utility. That has been a common miscon-struction, and many a child and school have been the worse for it. Learning to do all that may be useful, whether pleasing at the time or not, must surely be the better part of any education, or the whole of it; since doing simply as we please is the nega-tion of all training. For his own good our boy does many a thing he cannot relish at the moment; only he does nothing on our mere assertion that it will be good for him, nothing in which he cannot see the good himself. Other things may wait upon his understanding. Meanwhile he will be very busy with the things that fit his age.

Upon these, however, we may be far briefer. Not that Rousseau is the briefer with them, for he gives the positive education twice the space he has just given to the negative one; but the positive training, even at its most original, needs but little explanation. In assurance that it will be thorough in its kind, we may leave out nearly all detail and mention only a few leading principles.

The child may be taught anything worth learning that is now within his grasp. What is most worth learning must depend in part upon the given child. There is no one list for all, though there are certain things that ought to be in every list. But it is less important that he learn of many things than that his mastery of every given thing attempted shall be real. For the main aim is to bring him to proficiency in the kind of reasoning he can use.

In so saying, Rousseau has not forgotten that he called the child incapable of reason, and is careful to explain that he is using the same word in different senses. The child can do no reasoning of an abstract kind, but he can show all sorts of intelligence and ingenuity among the things around him. His head is full of images and empty of all real ideas; an image being a mental picture of an object in his world, and an idea being an intellection of the object in its various relations. Thus he will have a perfect knowledge of a falling stone long before he can have any notion of the law of gravitation. The most that he can do with images is to combine them into something we may call a simple idea, and the process of so doing comprises all the reasoning he can compass. It is a sort of *raison sensitive*. A man may use it too; but he may also work upon ideas themselves, combining simple ones into the composites which we call abstractions. And that is a process of the *raison intellectuelle*, or reason proper, which no child can have. Of course the two kinds of reasoning shade into each other, and our author calls the one the only basis for the other. That is why he would perfect the one against the other's coming.

So our boy will spend his whole time learning just as many facts and forming just as many simple ideas as he can truly master. That will be his positive education, and it will be thorough. We may cover a hundred pages of detail by saying that it all consists in making him a little expert in his world before he ever hears of laws and principles in force throughout it; to the end that he may really know the meaning of the laws in his own time because he has become an adept in the things they govern. To be such an adept is to be as self-reliant and as self-sufficient as his years allow. It is to be a natural child in a world of culture.

And Rousseau brings the boy of his dream into our presence. At the age of twelve, the lad is full of health and vigour, with no care or fear upon his brow. Lively but not restless, he is self-reliant and still modest. He is contented. In every word and act he is open and confident, but never vain or insolent. He is given to no aimless babbling or interrogation, and will never pester or monopolize us. He has none of the fine phrases that he might have memorized if we had thought them good for him, and he will say the simple truth out of his heart. He will never speak a needless syllable.

His notions are few and simple, but as clear as crystal. The little that he knows is truly his. He has not learned it from a master's word, but from his own experience as regulated by his master with a care of which he little dreams. If he reads a book more slowly than another boy, he will read the world more fluently. His wit is not upon his tongue, but in his brain. His judgement is far better than his memory. He can speak one language only, and but very simply, but he understands each word he utters.

Give him a command and he is at a loss to know your meaning, but ask for any reasonable thing of him and he will be as obliging as he can. In the same spirit he will ask of you or any one at need; not as if you owed him something, but as if he knew you would be kind. There will be no cringing in his request, neither any open or dissembled arrogance, but only a modest trust in your good-will. If his request is granted, he will show his pleasure by something better than a formal phrase, for he will feel he owes you something for your kindness. If it is denied, he will not insist or whine.

Leave him free and watch him. With no need to prove his liberty, since he has always had it, he will not be boisterous. He will move alertly to his purpose, but will never stir without one, and his every motion will show skill in shaping means to purposes. As he explores his world he will not be for ever plying you with queries, but will fairly do his best to find out his own answer. In a quandary he will be less disconcerted than another boy, and in danger less affrighted. In all proper matters he will be a leader. By the end of childhood he has made the most of the intelligence a child may have.

III

Such a boy will have a little time from now to adolescence when for once his strength is greater than his present need. Weaker than a man in bone and sinew, he has almost equal skill in his own sphere; and with his necessities provided for him, he is still as free from heavy duties as from the distracting passions that will soon be on him. So he has a residue of energy to store up wisdom for the strain to come. The time is one for study.

It is brief, and study is illimitable. The boy may learn the faster if we have delayed till he is ready, but at best there are more things than he will ever master. Some of them are false, and some will serve no end but pride, while some are still beyond his understanding. But even when we put aside all these, there are more left than we can hope to teach. How are we to choose among them?

There can be but one choice. We must teach him the most useful. Of course we are not thinking of the most lucrative, and we shall have no need to use the latter term; but in any proper sense utility will be the test of what he ought to know, for there can be no greater reason for his learning what is useless than for doing any other useless thing. If this be another truism, we may ask how well we honour it in the average education. And if in clinging to it here we fail to teach our boy certain matters more or less familiar to his fellows, we may remember that we did not start a book on education to propose precisely what was being done. We are trying to train a mind, and not to cram it—to perfect a mental instrument rather than to crowd a reservoir of erudition.

And the boy himself must see the use of what he learns. So far we have had to keep him in the path by mere necessity because we have had no means to tell him of our motive, but as soon as he begins to see the use of things we must let him find his own way, with all proper aid, as far as possible. So in choosing studies for him we must train him more and more to test their use in his own right and choose them for himself. Later he will have another principle for any choice of action in the final test of right and wrong; but the test of right and wrong is still too far beyond him, while that of usefulness is now coming well within his ken.

His natural curiosity will give an ample motive for his learning and our teaching. But we must be very sure that it is natural, and not of artificial growth. So long as he is bent on simply finding out the most he can about the things around him he is in the proper path, but as soon as he begins to covet learning for the sake of seeming wise in his own generation he has drifted into pride. By all means we must keep him out of its mazes. For no sort of emulation should be known to him, nor any curiosity born of vanity. If he were all alone upon an island, he would set about the study of it just as fast as possible, and never pause for self-comparison or reference to the prejudice and error of the world beyond; he would look for nothing but the useful. That is just the spirit in which we would have him learn the actual world he lives in; he may then be better fitted for a reckoning with its prejudice and error later. In that spirit we may stimulate his curiosity by all proper means, and there are plenty without emulation.

We shall stimulate it all the more if we refrain from sating it. If we satisfy it every instant we shall only deaden it, but if we have the gift to keep it busy for a happy hour finding out a thing we could reveal at any moment, we may kindle it to many a further search. Meanwhile the thing in question will be really learned. And never mind if fewer things are learned in this way, though there need be little fear of that; we are educators, and not crammers. For that reason we shall teach the boy the least we can, and make him learn the most. We may all too easily tell him what he ought to know, and so train him to wait for us to do his work. We may far more wisely make him a discoverer.

The more he learns about utility, the readier he will be to do unpleasant things for his own good. But he must see the good in them before the action will evince the self-control that makes for character. If he does them merely by command, he is but proving the control of some one else. We would therefore never have him do a thing against his will, though we would have him do all sorts of things unpleasant to him at the moment but of useful promise. So we shall give him no command as such. If we cannot show him that a given thing is useful, we can probably delay it; or if not, we had better fall back on the kind of force that we have hitherto employed.

Such will be the spirit of our teaching. We shall lay down no one list of things to teach, but rather show the way the spirit ought to work in all the things that may seem wise. For a few examples we may start with what is just before the boy's eye.

Among the first things that will strike his eye and stir his curiosity will be the ground beneath him and the sun and stars above. So his earliest glances may be in the direction of geography and of astronomy. Such would hardly be the case if we meant to start with books and maps and planispheres, for these are made for rather older heads. But if we are starting with the things themselves, the natural order is to take the ones that fill his eye first. There is no one object that will be more striking than the sun. Instigated by us just as far as may be wise, he will watch the action of the sun until he knows exactly what it does from day to day; and aided by us just as little as is possible, he will try to find out what can make it come up every day and go down every night, though never in the same spot and never at the same time. Once he has puzzled out the reason, he will really know it; he may then go on the faster with the moon and stars, and with the further problems in his reach. For his geography he may well start with two familiar spots at a reasonable distance from each other which he has often covered. He will make a map of his own trip, and gradually fill in all the intervening points; then he will expand it and perfect it till it makes a picture of all the world that he has seen. Doubtless his own map will be less accurate and beautiful than one that we could make or buy for him, but he will have learned more in the drawing of it and will be far readier to see the meaning in the maps of worlds he does not know. In the same way he will start his physics with experiments on the things around him for a laboratory. With a little aid, for instance, he will soon be making his own compass; and rude as it may be, it will mean more for him than the finest specimen that we could get him from a shop.

And so with all his other instruments, and all his other studies; these are illustrations merely, and are much abbreviated. In this spirit he should master all the useful things he can, but only in this spirit should he learn the least of them. And the three essentials for the proper spirit are that he must start from his own curiosity, must go on from his own sense of value, and must conquer by his own exertion. Then his learning will be real. We shall have our hands full in encouraging and guiding him, and we need not try to force him further than the proper spirit warrants. As we should not, so we cannot really force a curiosity or sense of value on him. If a rational stimulation fails, we may be sure that an irrational one will do no better.

But so far our examples have all come from things, and he is now to learn a little of the more perplexing world of man. To show him something of the social order and his place in it without imparting any of its prejudices is about the hardest duty we shall have. But at least we may begin as usual in the simplest way. We can do no better than to lead him straight among the toilers of the world and let him watch the interplay of industry in shop and mine and factory, with the mutual dependence of all men beneath the social bond. He will soon infer that every man must bear a part.

Some of his opinions may be novel at his entrance to the world of man. He will value men, as he has always valued things, according to their simple usefulness. Just as he has always seen more good in glass and iron than in diamond and gold, he will find the glazier and the smith more estimable than the jeweller. He will have no notion that the fame of men is often in the inverse ratio of their usefulness, and he would need a lengthy lesson in the ways of prejudice to find out why. We shall give him no such lesson now. If we tell him all the ways of prejudice at present, he will fall as straight into them as another boy, but if we keep him free of them till he can meet them on the ground of reason, he will have a fairer chance to make up his account with them.

For a single instance, we may see what we must tell him of the use of money in the interplay of industry. We may easily show him how it was invented as a single unit of exchange to replace a clumsy scheme of barter, and with that we shall have told him all its use. But we need not tell him it has been abused until the love of it has been called the root of all evil. We need not try to show him how the possession of it and of the things it buys has come to pass for honour, or why the prizes of the world go oftener to the men of wealth than to the men of worth. He will be the better in an innocence as yet of such a shame. Even if we had to teach him pride, we need not start him in its meanest form.

Far from hoping for a life of wealth and ease, our boy will rather wish to fit himself for his own part in the great game of industry that he is watching. For he will see that every man should have a part—that every one must owe a debt to all who work for which his own work is the only payment. We have seen the kind of part our boy will consider useful, and we cannot possibly do better than to honour his opinion by allowing him to learn a trade. He may well become a carpenter. If he happens to be rich, he is to be no little gentleman at play with carpentry, but is to learn the trade like any boy who may expect to spend a life at it. He will stoop to the estate of artisan in order to rise above his own. But even here we must look out for pride. He must not be vain of his humility, or he will only have found another way of being proud. To be proud of mastering a prejudice is only one more way of hugging prejudice.

In his own inventions and discoveries he will now have trained his judgement to a point where it is about to flower into reason. All our care has been to bring it wisely to that point. We have been training him to work like a peasant in order that he may think like a philosopher and not be idle like a savage. He is past the time when he could deal with nothing more than images, and is now at work with ideas also; and with these his judgement enters on its office. Now an image is the product of sensation merely, and it cannot but be right. When our eye reports that a straight stick partly under water appears crooked, it is telling us the literal truth; it can have no way to lie about an image. But an idea comes from a comparison of two or more sensations, and the act of judgement it involves, though of the simplest, may be wrong. Only when we say the stick is really crooked have we made an error. And this holds for all sensations and for every judgement; all our errors are of judgement, or arise in the formation of ideas. That is why we have been so careful of the way in which our boy formed them.

The easy thing to do about the stick is to pull it out of the water and let him see that it is straight, with a word or two about refraction which we need hardly hope will be within his grasp. The easy thing is usually to do all his work for him and to tell him all we care for him to know. But it is no way to train his judgement. The wiser thing will be to see that he finds out about the stick by watching the bend in it alter if he goes around it, turn into a zigzag if he stirs the water, descend and disappear if he drains off the tub, and do various other things to put him on the track of truth and lead him duly to a notion of something like refraction. The illustration is the simplest, and it may be tedious; but it holds for any kind of training we shall give his judgement. We are not so much to teach him truths as to fit him to discover truth. When we shall have done it, we shall have him at the gate of reason.

IV

We have brought our boy to adolescence in two aims. In the negative education we have tried to keep him free of any prejudice about the world of man in order that he may now face its problems in the light of reason. In the positive education we have done our best to fit his reason for a reckoning with the problems and with all the prejudices that must come along with them. For his final study must be man. It will lead, for instance, into history for the record of what man has been, as into politics and ethics for the ideal of what he ought to be; into metaphysics for such genuine truth as he may hope to know, and into religion for assurance of his final destiny.

The strongest of the passions comes upon our boy just as he is rising into reason, and without our watchful care will make submission to the reason difficult indeed. As a natural necessity, the passion cannot but be good, and all ascetic notions of suppressing it must be as indefensible as they are vain; but there is little need to say that its abuses are as vicious as is any other thing that artifice has brought upon us. A supreme example of all that we have said about the use and the abuse of any natural gift, the strongest of our passions is the most transmutable of all. For even as it may be elevated into the purest human love that we may know, it may also fall into perversions into which the very brutes would never stray. In our artificial world there is great danger that it will be roused before its time by lewd suggestion or by smirking secrecy, and that instead of any natural awakening of the imagination by the senses there will be an artificial stimulation of the sense by the imagination. For precaution we may keep our boy innocent of any knowledge of the instinct until its arrival, and thus properly retard its coming.

With it comes a great if gradual expansion of the boy's general sensibility. He begins to feel a kind of sympathy for others such as he has never really known before. For hitherto he has enjoyed no feeling but a child's, just as he has known no other understanding; and the feeling of a child is quite as different from a man's as is his reasoning. Only as he understands enough to put himself into another's place will he come to feel the joy or sorrow of another. So we must train his understanding and his sympathy in concert, each to aid the other to perfect a moral being in whom they shall be at one. We may know our boy has come into an understanding of the world of man when he has found his true place in it, and into morality if he is content in his own place; if he keeps unspotted from the prejudices of the world, or free from pride.

If we would train his sentiment in unison with reason, we may best begin by making him familiar with the average lot of man. We shall not hurry him into a proud society of lords and princelings or into the haunts of wealth and power. For superior fortune is too likely to arouse his envy and ambition, while affliction will more probably call up the sympathy that we would cultivate in him. We shall therefore start by showing him the common lot of suffering humanity, as seen rather in the men of poorer fortune than in those of higher favour. We need go to no extreme in a display of anguish such as would but overwhelm the sensibility we are endeavouring to educate; we may avoid the lazar-house at one pole as we pass the palace at the other. There will be enough of pity in the average lot to train his sympathy into the rational benevolence which is its end. And in this way he will begin to know his fellows, as is right, by what is common to them. He will not start with envious distinctions between lord and peasant, between heir and pauper, or with any of the artificial inequalities that loom so large in our sophisticated eyes but are so little in comparison with the common fate of all mankind. By the common fate that is the natural and fairly equal lot of all men will he first come to know his fellows. Then the earliest expansion of his sympathy for them will be fairly free of pride and prejudice; and he will be the readier for a reckoning in turn with their artificial inequalities.

As he goes on to such inequalities he will come into the maze of social prejudice through which he must finally thread his way. He must learn all that the men of this world have become in the entangled web of artifice. And the sympathy

he has been gathering for their natural lot will have some
rude shocks as he finds out the unnatural ways into which they
have fallen. If we would still have him pity them and not
despise them, if we would still keep him free from pride in
any sense of his superiority to them, we may better show
him their unnatural ways afar off; not in the men in his
own circle, but in those so distant from him as to lure him into
no invidious comparison with them. The wise course would
be to place him among men who would inspire only love and
sympathy, and yet to show him others afar off who have fallen
into vice and error such as would excite his scorn and hatred
if he met them face to face. And there is a way to do this—a
study that will show him all the sins and follies of his kind at a
sufficient distance to evoke his pity rather than his pride and
scorn. The time has come for history.

There are difficulties in the study even now. Historians
tend to overstate the evil man has done, and to underrate the
good, because they deal so largely with the catastrophes that
show him at his worst. So the annals of the race are more or
less a calumny upon it. And at best the facts of history must
take on some distortion in their passage through the historian's
mind, while at the worst they may lose all real resemblance to
what actually happened. Accordingly the best historian for our
boy, other things equal, will be the one who does the least
interpreting; who presents the facts and lets the boy find the
meaning. That is why the ancients are superior to the moderns,
though in varying degrees. Sallust and Polybius are too fond
of colouring their portraits, and Tacitus may better wait for
later years; Thucydides is best in giving us the facts and leaving
us to find the lessons in them. Unluckily he deals with war
perhaps the least instructive part of history; and on this coun
Herodotus might serve us better if his simplicity were not so
often near to puerility. But all our histories deal too much with
the unusual and with men upon parade, and our boy should
learn about the men and the events of every day. So the best
of history is biography, since it will serve better in this way.
Here again the ancients still surpass the moderns, for they are
freer from the false canons of decorum that forbid the revelation of the real man. And the best of all biographers is Plu-

tarch, in whose words our boy will find more lessons about man than in any other written record.

We shall need all our imagination to conceive the lessons such a boy will see in his new learning. In his freedom from the prejudices which have overlain us all our lives and smothered so much of our sympathy and rational opinion, in his privilege of looking on the record of his race in the pure light of reason, what will be his wonder, what his shame and pity, as the curtain rises on the follies of his fellows through the centuries of their unlovely annals! What distress as he beholds them murdering and tormenting one another at the call of an ambition to chase shadows, of a pride that lures them out of nature into every discontent! And what grief as he learns that so pitifully few of all the men in history have found the simple secret of their happiness and duty in clinging to the place that nature meant for them!

So inured are we to the ways of pride and prejudice that the story of our annals has lost nearly all its mournful meaning for us. We can pass over the inquiry that Cyneas put to Pyrrhus, with a thousand matters like it, as an outworn epigram. Why will you go on slaughtering and enslaving peoples, O Pyrrhus, when all your conquests so far are only so many torments to you? We can read the question over and pass on. But our boy will read it with a difference. He will take it as a simple verity which any Pyrrhus should have known and lived by long before he reached the age of twenty. To prepare the boy to read the question, and all others like it, in this way has been our purpose with him all along.

In a similar spirit he will enter upon all his other studies in the world of man, and we may omit the long details. The time for history is the time for fables, for the reason given in deferring them from a tenderer age. It is the time for art and literature, and for the development of taste. It is the time for social science, or the formal study of the way for individuals to live a corporate life. For such study the boy is presented with the substance of the *Social Contract*, which remains for our perusal in the chapter following. And among other matters it is finally the time for the most important thing of all—for religion, and for ethics and metaphysics as involved therein.

In our author, metaphysical inquiry is virtually confined to matters that will have an ethical importance, and the two are linked inseparably with religion. So he tells the boy all he has to say about the three in the *Profession* of his Vicar, to be treated in our closing chapter.

There is much more in his treatise than has been suggested here, but his general plan and purpose are now clear to us. There is an impressive moment when he tells the boy all he has been trying to do for him from the cradle, and explains how and why he lived so long under a protecting force, how he then came under the guidance of the canon of utility, and how he is at last to be a moral agent, free to choose as his instruction should have fitted him for choice. One of his choices is that of the mate which whom he is to pass his life, and a lengthy fifth book of *Emile* is devoted to her own education. But it is pretty well agreed that Rousseau is unhappier in his idea of a woman's education than in any other portion of his book, if not of his entire work. It is possibly the one idea in which he is a strong reactionary. And if we are dealing with the Rousseau who is still alive in our day, we may omit all further reference to his plan for the instruction of a woman, for it is as dead as is his scheme of musical notation.

V

'The sight of a boy in fetters, upon the day of my first putting on the blue clothes, was not exactly fitted to assuage the natural terrors of initiation. I was of tender years, barely turned of seven; and had only read of such things in books, or seen them but in dreams. I was told he had *run away*. This was the punishment for the first offence.—As a novice I was soon after taken to see the dungeons. These were little, square, Bedlam cells, where a boy could just lie at his length upon straw and a blanket—a mattress, I think, was afterwards substituted—with a peep of light, let in askance, from a prison-orifice at top, barely enough to read by. Here the poor boy was locked in by himself all day, without sight of any but the porter who brought him his bread and water—who *might not speak to him*;—or of the beadle, who came twice a week to call him out to receive his periodical chastisement, which was almost welcome, because it separated him for a brief interval from solitude;—and here he was shut up by himself *of nights*, out of the reach of any sound, to suffer whatever horrors the weak nerves, and superstition incident to his time of life, might subject him to. This was the penalty for the second offence. Wouldst thou like, Reader, to see what became of him in the next degree?'

'The culprit, who had been a third time an offender, and whose expulsion was at this time deemed irreversible, was brought forth, as at some solemn *auto-da-fé*, arrayed in uncouth and most appalling attire, all trace of his late 'watchet-weeds' carefully effaced, he was exposed in a jacket, resembling those which London lamplighters formerly delighted in, with a cap of the same. The effect of this divestiture was such as the ingenious devisers of it could have anticipated. With his pale and frightened features, it was as if some of those disfigurements in Dante had seized upon him. In this disguisement he was brought into the hall, where awaited him the whole number of his schoolfellows, whose joint lessons and sports he was thenceforth to share no more; the awful presence of the steward, to be seen for the last time; of the executioner beadle, clad in his state robe for the occasion; and of two faces more, of direr import, because never but in these extremities visible. These were governors; two of whom, by choice, or charter, were always accustomed to officiate at these *Ultima Supplicia*; not to mitigate (so at least we understood it), but to enforce the uttermost stripe. Old Bamber Gascoigne, and Peter Aubert, I remember, were colleagues on one occasion, when the beadle turning rather pale, a glass of brandy was ordered to prepare him for the mysteries. The scourging was, after the old Roman fashion, long and stately. The lictor accompanied the criminal quite round the hall. We were generally too faint with attending to the previous disgusting circumstances to make accurate report with our eyes of the degree of corporal suffering inflicted. Report, of course, gave out the back knotty and livid. . . .'[1]

This was not an everyday occurrence, but it happened on occasion; in the present case the scene of revel was the famous hospital entitled Christ's. Not to look on the event as other than an occasional episode of education in our author's period, is it any wonder that so many men from his own century to ours have hailed him as the liberator of the child? But if his system is the better understood by contrast with the one prevailing prior to it, it cannot be justified by such comparison alone. That it superseded something bad is not enough to prove it good, and we must have another reason for endorsing or condemning it.

We may say that in omitting many portions of *Emile* we have also left out most of its incidental inconsistencies and all of its minor absurdities. For there are certain notions in it that deserve no other name, and they had better be dismissed before we ask the value of its main proposal. Nearly all of them occur in the notorious 'examples' which our author sometimes

[1] Lamb, *Christ's Hospital Five and Thirty Years Ago.*

offered for the illustration of his ideas, and in which he very rightly feared that he would be at his unhappiest. So we have been silent on such matters as the famous conspiracy with Farmer Robert to give the boy a notion of the rights of property, or the further plot with the magician to show him manners and discretion. These are not the main things, and the doctrine stands or falls without them. And whatever inconsistencies may lurk in it as here reviewed, we need hardly say that it is an essential unity and in essential consonance with its author's fundamental principles as previously explained. So firmly does it rest upon those principles as to give him reason for remarking that *Emile* is less a manual of education than a treatise on the natural goodness of our species.

Some of the more common criticisms of his plan were canvassed in preparing for our statement of it. In substance they object to it as an ideal out of all attainment, and the answer to them is that it was meant for nothing else. The only question is whether it is better worth approximating than another plan. But before we ask the final question we must still clear up a few misunderstandings that would cloud the issue.

There is no intent to make the boy a libertine. It has been contended that the precious liberty demanded for him will habituate him only to indulgence of his own desire, and that all his ethical career will start and end in doing as he pleases. If that is true, our treatise is pernicious and we may have done with it; but at least no such intention is discoverable in its pages. Safeguarded in the right at first by our unslumbering force, and then inured to every act that will be useful and to none of any other kind, the boy is meant to reach maturity in a submission to the moral law that will involve unusual renunciation of desire. We would have all his submission voluntary, to be sure; but only because we cannot think of any other kind as equally desirable, because we cannot think of character in any terms but those of self-control.

There is no intent to make him an automaton. It has been equally objected that the absolute control of every moment in his life will leave him none of the freedom that has just been found essential. The answer is that while our author holds it necessary to remain in absolute control, at least through childhood, he would also leave the boy feeling wholly free; and that he has his own device to gain the two ends. Of a surety, the device will take unusual care and wisdom to employ, but at least there is no purpose in it to make the boy a machine. And to both these criticisms we should say that in our author's mind there is no necessary conflict between freedom and control, as we shall find again when he discusses liberty and law in the ideal state.

There is no intent to charm the boy into education by some sort of artificial fascination. It has been objected that if all his acts are to be voluntary we shall have to tax our wit to find ingenious ways of coaxing his volition. But there is no such intention, if only for the reason that it would no longer be volition, but a mere surrender to enticement. The boy is reared under the stern rule of necessity, of utility, and of the moral law; and if these succeed in winning his devotion, it is not because they have been decorated in false colours for him, but because they have been shown him in their true validity. It might be hard to say whether our author would have more deplored an education by compulsion or an education by cajolery. In his period the main method was compulsion, and we have his protest; but we have his equal protest against the artificial fascination that has frequently been substituted by his own mistaken followers. He found the teacher of his day doing too much of the pupil's work by way of forcing education on him; he advised the teacher to be no less busy seeing that the pupil got an education by his own exertion; and he left many a teacher overworking to find ways of charming pupils into such exertion. But that is something which he would have disapproved as much as any other artificial stimulation.

There is finally no intent to give a single boy so unusual a training as to make him a mere oddity and possibly a martyr in the world as it now is. It could certainly be objected that if there were only one Emile in an alien society he would suffer a sad fate for eccentricity, and probably to little purpose; hardly would he even be allowed to raise a question whether he or the whole regiment was out of step. But we are not told to train a single Emile for an alien freak in our poor world; we are told that we shall have a better world when it is all peopled with Emiles. And the one real question is whether that is true.

From the outset we have said the question would be opened at this point, but hardly that it would be answered. We are trying to set down our author's doctrine, and would rather leave its value for the reader to determine. The reader will encounter very varying opinions on it if he cares to look into the teeming books and essays that discuss it. He will find that it is 'not worth a shrug of the shoulders'[1] and that it 'would abolish all moral training;[2]' he will also find that it is 'the most beautiful, the most thorough, and the most suggestive educational treatise ever written.'[3] And since he will find every sort of intermediate verdict, we may spare him the intrusion of another here. But since he will discover everywhere that the doctrine has had a far greater influence than any other educational theory, and that with all its ideality it is at least practical enough to have become the main foundation for the schools and colleges in nearly all the world to-day, he may possibly be driven to make up his own mind as to whether it is mainly good or evil. And it may assist him to repeat some of the terms in which he will make up his mind. If he is persuaded that a child should be a child in tender years, that we should force as little of our own will as is possible upon him, that we should teach him nothing until he can fully understand it, that we should teach him mainly from experience in preference to books, and indeed that we should teach him the very least we can and make him learn the most; if he thinks that we should strive for judgement rather than for learning, and for character before intelligence, he will come to the conclusion that our author must be mainly in the right. There may well be two opinions upon many of these matters, and conceivably upon them all. So there is no need for quick decision; but the terms in which we must decide are clear.

[1] Lasserre, le Romantisme français, p. 68.
[2] James Welton, Encyclopaedia Britannica, vii. 969.
[3] Lanson, Histoire de la Littérature française, 14th ed., p. 796.

III
THE NATURAL SOCIETY

CERTAIN evils in the state of Venice set our author planning an elaborate treatise of political philosophy as early as 1743. All he ever published of it went into the *Social Contract* in 1762. In the nineteen years of interim he had pondered the political philosophers before him and had also written several essays that reveal the gradual progress of his thinking toward his final theory. By 1753 he was on his way to it in the *Discourse on Inequality*, too often thought to contradict it, and two years later he put nearly all the gist of it into his article upon 'Political Economy' in the *Encyclopaedia*; and naturally enough, since in the year preceding he had apparently drawn up the first draft of the *Contract* itself, as preserved in the Geneva manuscript.[1] For a time after his retirement from Paris two years later, he was much intent on the completion of the work, but as the other labours of the extraordinary period following gained upon him more and more, he faltered at the magnitude of his original plan; so he finished what we have in the *Social Contract*, and gave up the rest.

If only a fragment of his first plan, however, the *Contract* is a unit all alone, and is the heart of his political theory; and though he may have said in old age that it was open to revision, he unquestionably held its essence for his final doctrine. Witness a summary he made of it for the political instruction of Emile, and another written in his own defence in the *Letters from the Mount*; witness also his later efforts to adapt it to actual practice, with allowance for the necessary exigencies, in the *Plan of a Constitution for Corsica* (1765) and the *Considerations on the Government of Poland* (1772). These make altogether a fair body of political doctrine, and may all be laid under incidental levy in our discussion of the main treatise.

[1] First published by Alexeieff, Moscow, 1887; later by Dreyfus-Brisac in his edition of the *Contrat social*, Paris, 1896, and by Vaughan in *The Political Writings of Jean-Jacques Rousseau*, Cambridge, 1915.

The treatise is so different from most of Rousseau's work that many men have called it incompatible with nearly all the rest. To them the other work is an outpouring of emotion at the expense of reason, or even to its intentional discredit, while this is so compact of reasoning as hardly to admit a trace of sentiment, and is indeed of such immitigable logic in the abstract as to seem inspired at times by a sheer love of formal symmetry; the very style employed being about the opposite of the author's usual manner. And many further contradictions have been listed. In the other works, for instance, freedom is a great necessity for man, while here the last vestige of his freedom is surrendered to the state. In the others, to say all at once, nature is the ideal and society the irremediable lapse from it, while here the ideal is a society that will take us for ever out of sight of nature.

We have tried to show already that the other work is something more than simple sentiment. There is enough of that, assuredly, and often out of season; but the *Emile* will not pass as an emotional classic and even the *New Heloise* is no undiluted flood of passion. We have also tried to show how our author meant all sentiment to be at peace with reason. If the *Social Contract* is plain logic, it is because he took this for the medium proper to the subject and because he had a notable and sometimes all but fatal turn for logic too. We shall find him still devoted to the cause of freedom; not, however, to that lowest form of freedom which is the independence open only to a man who knows no government, but to the higher kind which is the liberty known only under law and earned only in willing obedience to it. And we shall also find that the natural man is still his one ideal, but in the full development which can come only in the right society. The *Contract* is the picture of such a society.

In its way it is therefore a Utopia ; it is for the state exactly what *Emile* is for the school. But there are at least two kinds of Utopia. In the one, the people are so perfect and their situation so ideal that they can need no cunning polity to get along in bliss; be but a Houyhnhnm, and you may ignore the art of politics. But such an ideal is a pure phantasm because it is not in our nature. In the other, the people are human beings in an average environment, and they may aim at a Utopia only through the most consummate social art. The aim will still be an ideal, but not a phantasm; for though they may never attain it, they may come nearer and nearer to it because it is proper to their nature. Rousseau's Utopia is of the second kind. He does not expect us to reach it, but he believes that we can approach it, and that such is our only hope; and he so believes because he has done his utmost to derive it from our very nature. In this it is at one with all his work.

Even with the *Discourse on Inequality*, so often held annihilative to the *Social Contract*, there is no real contradiction. In the *Inequality* he had shown how men may have first rambled into a society with consequences largely evil, and in the *Contract* he shows how they may now create a society with altogether good results. In the first he was answering as best he could the question as to how they came to form the first society, while in the second he is trying to show how they may now form the best one. The earlier societies have left us a long list of woes, and the question now is whether there can be any society that will rid us of them. He believes that he has found one under the Social Pact. For the Social Pact is not, as commonly supposed, a thing that we all signed long ago to start the first society; it is what we must sign now if we are to have the right one. It is not history, but may some day be history.

So much is clear, though nearly always misinterpreted, from the first words of the *Contract*. 'Man is born free, but everywhere he is in chains.' If Rousseau had not sought a fiery epigram to open nearly every book, he might have saved us a good deal of printer's ink and bad blood ; but he means only that there was a time when we were independent because as yet we knew no society and that now we have all come under some sort of social rule. 'How did the change come about? *I do not know.*' I made the best guess I could in my book on *Inequality*, but even there I called it only a conjecture. 'What can make the change *legitimate?* That question I believe I can answer.' I think I know the kind of society that is just and right; nor am I recanting my former Discourse if I too plan a Utopia. Let us see what it will be.

I

The one society of nature's making is the family. The authority of parents is a natural necessity as long as it is requisite for the preservation of their children. Beyond that point, if continued, it is voluntarily accepted; so no other society can grow even out of this one save by some sort of agreement.

Every other society is of man's contriving. It can therefore get authority only from the men who make it; and the authority, to be legitimate, can rest only on an agreement among the men.

In vain shall we seek to rest it upon any other thing. Many a philosopher has based it upon force ; but force gives only power, not authority. No doubt force has often conferred mastery, and so inspired the famous doctrine of the 'right of the strongest'. But force may do almost any other thing except create a right. If we simply yield to force, it is because we must, never because we ought; and our meekest submission can imply no moral obligation. Even though a single man enslave the world, obedience to him will prove any other thing than duty to obey. So the doctrine of the right of the strongest, however illustrious in its apologists, is a simple contradiction in terms. By no alchemy of political philosophy can might make right.

So an agreement of the members is the only basis for authority in a society. And if we now ask what species of agreement will be right for them, we must look for its terms in the purposes that lead the men to make it. Each of them will give up freedom to the group only in the desire to secure the corporate support, but each will still desire to save as much of his own freedom as is possible withal. The two desires will be universal, and the agreement must provide some reconciliation for them ; so the problem of the individual and the state is with us at the start. But if the motives prompting the agreement will be universal, the agreement that will meet them must be universal also; and there will be one right agreement only, or one rational basis for society in any time or place. Of course societies may differ in all manner of detail, as we shall see, but every rational one must rest at bottom on the single Social Pact that is legitimate. Now if we fully phrase the motives of men entering such a pact, we shall be asking for a society which shall support each member with all the common power, but in which each member, though united with all others in a mutual dependence, shall yet be at liberty. If any pact can do these seemingly conflicting things, it will surely be the right one. And there is one pact only that will answer. It may vary in the phrasing, but in bare essentials it will always provide that:

'Each of us gives his person and his total power to the common cause, under the supreme authority of the general will, and we receive every member as an integral part of our group.'[1]

It will take a good while to show how these bare terms will do all we have asked of them—how they will endow us with the power of the group and yet leave us at liberty. But we are here reducing our pact to the minimum that is essential in whatever time or place, and most of what is left to say will be an expansion of its terms to show that they imply and provide all we are asking. Before we are through we may find that any man surrendering his all upon such terms will of necessity be free. But a good deal of discussion is required to reach that point, and we may begin more modestly.

Each man gives his all to the society on terms equal for all men; and if the terms are truly equal, no man can wish to make them tyrannical, for he will be as much afflicted by them as will any one. Each man acquires over all the others the same power he surrenders to them, and thus recovers the equivalent of what he loses; but he inherits the additional strength of the whole group.[2] And with the birth of the society, the individuals in it undergo important changes, moral and material. Hitherto the best they have enjoyed in material things has been a perilous *possession* of what they dared to call their own, while now they will receive a right of *property* in all their goods—a word that

[1] iii. 313.
[2] The statement has given a good deal of trouble. It may be clearest in a homely illustration. When there was no society, of course I paid no taxes, and now I have to do so. That is my loss. But all the other members also pay taxes, and the amount of their tribute that is used for my own benefit should equal the amount I pay to benefit them all. So my gain is equal to my loss. But together we can do things with our taxes that would be impossible in any other way; so by joining forces we have each inherited a power hitherto unknown. Extend the illustration, and the principle would seem to hold. Every duty that I owe the other members of society is balanced by a duty they perform in part for my own benefit; and meanwhile we have all gained the strength that comes from union.

has no meaning until there is a society to give it one. The moral transformation will be greater still. Hitherto they may have suffered more or less from the natural inequalities among them, but now they will come into a civil equality in which all men have the same rights under the law. Hitherto each of them has followed his own desire, but now desire is superseded by the moral principle that rises only when they enter into their agreement. Of course they must lose something in surrendering uncharted independence for a moral life. But we have seen that the pure freedom to follow their desire is only slavery to the desire; and in rising to an ethical principle they have gained so much more than they have lost that, if the abuses of their new estate do not degrade them below their former level, they must for ever bless the moment that delivered them out of their brute independence into law and liberty.

The power that makes the law is sovereign in the state. For the right state we have said it is the *general will*. But hardly any term is oftener misused or calls for clearer explanation. Of course it means that no one man or group can have supreme authority, for we have seen that all authority must rest on an agreement of the people. Any authority entrusted to an individual must come from them, and they will always remain sovereign over him. Of course it therefore means that the people rule, but it also means something far less vague. For in what sense do we say the people rule? Unless they are unanimous, as very seldom, some of them will always be going against their own will in obedience to the rest; so why not say that only some of them can rule? If they were unanimous, the *will of all* would be the sovereign, but this is virtually impossible. And we have taken one step toward a definition of the general will in saying that it can hardly ever be the will of all the people.

At any moment the members of the state may entertain a mass of more or less conflicting aims which cannot all be met. Now we may first put aside all aims so purely personal that they can have no bearing on the common cause. These the sovereign will let alone, as things of no concern; for it is not thinkable that any one will take the trouble to interfere in matters totally indifferent. Whether I eat flesh or fish, or whether I wear blue or black, the sovereign can seldom care; and so in thousands of such matters where I have a large realm of liberty at once. When I give the state my ' all ', it is implicit in the nature of the case that I give only 'all' that matters to the state. The rest remains to me, and is established for me by no mere convention, for the sovereign is supreme over conventions, but simply by the nature of the case. Only I must realize that in imaginable exigencies almost anything may come to have a bearing on the common cause and an interest for the sovereign. Whether I eat flesh may be the state's concern in some emergency when there is not enough to go around, and even whether I wear blue may be of public interest if some chemist finds that certain dye-stuffs spread disease. And I should finally realize that if there is any question whether a given thing concerns the common cause or not, the sovereign only may decide. In that sense I have indeed given up my all. It is not for me to dispute the sovereign in any matter; but it is in the nature of the sovereign to leave me free in many things.

Over and above all this, however, every member of the state will have a set of aims for the community at large. These will often conflict also, and cannot all be realized. If we simply added all of them together, we should have the will of all, and this would be the general will, as noted, only in the rare event of unanimity. Indeed, if we imagine it perpetually unanimous, we shall see at once that it could hardly be a will at all. For just as an individual with a single motive would act on it without any exercise of will or any notion that he had one, so a state whose members were always unanimous would act as an automaton and never know it owned a will at all. And if an individual with several motives simply added all of them together, he would still have nothing to act on; he would have only a sum of more or less conflicting motives, and he could not act until he had compared and contrasted them to find out where his highest interest seemed to lie. Even so a community that merely added up its aims would have only the amorphous will of all; but if it allows them to fuse and work on one another till the more or less conflicting ones are neutralized, it will have left a common element which the group believes to be its dominant aim. That aim is the general will. It is the sovereign. It is the only principle that we shall come to if we think out our assertion that the people rule. There is no other instrument by which they may do so.

But is this any more than a very abstract way of saying that some of us will rule while others will obey? If my will is neutralized, in part or wholly, in the process of discovering the general one, am I not in so far under bondage? And what is the difference between surrendering to what we call the general will and giving in to any group of other men?

In part the answer lies in the conditions necessary to create a general will. These are four, and they are all implicit in the pact with which we started. The pact was an ideal one, again, and we did not mean that it would work perfectly; but for the perfect general will it implied the four conditions. The will must count the vote of every man, or otherwise some men are making law for others. So much was implied when every member was received as an 'integral part of our group'. The will must obligate all members equally; it cannot be general if it favours or disfavours one or more of them. And such equality was stipulated when each man gave his all into the common cause. The will must deal only with that common cause, and not with any private interest. As soon as it touches individual interest it ceases to be general; for though many members act upon the personal concern of very few, or even all the rest on that of only one, the will must lack the voice of the few or one. It can therefore treat the public cause alone, and must be general in its purposes as well as in its composition. But above all it must be voiced by voters bent upon the common weal and willing to forget their own concerns; it will be perfect in proportion as they vote in pure devotion to the public good and in oblivion to their personal interest. To some extent they do so wherever they vote at all—as when they vote for taxes which any one of them would rather not have to pay. Only in a great extension of such public spirit does Rousseau see the way to a truly general will; and in search of such a spirit he often turns from the Paris of his day, where tyranny had stifled most of it, to the best records of such states as Rome and Sparta. The Spartan mother rushes upon the runner bringing news of the battle.[1] 'Your five sons are killed.' 'Vile slave, was it this I asked thee?' 'We have gained the victory!' And the mother hastens to the temple to give thanks to the gods. There was a citizen! True or mythical, the story is a supreme example of the public spirit necessary to the general will and to the healthy state. It was a solemn act to give our all into the common cause *under the supreme authority of the general will.* But if we are to look for liberty a little later, we must keep remembering that we gave our *all.*

The sovereignty is inalienable. It cannot be conferred on any individual or party, or it is no longer vested in the general will. The pact so stipulates because an individual may seek his own good at the common cost, and so may any party; only the general will is of its nature free from such temptation. Any will that is so tempted is no longer general. Of course we shall see later that the general will may empower officers to execute its plans, and may give them any title that seems fitting; but they will be its agents only, not the sovereign. 'The moment there is a master, there is no longer a sovereign.'[2]

By the like token, the sovereignty is indivisible. It cannot be split up among individuals or groups, each sovereign in a given sphere—among legislative and executive bodies, for example, or home and foreign offices. All such bodies are but agencies to carry out its plans, and may be very necessary; but back of all of them the sovereign is one and indivisible, and they are but its emanations.

In a sense the general will is infallible. It cannot but desire the common good, and in this it is at once superior to an individual ruler, who may indeed pursue his own advantage at the common cost. But of course it may mistake its own good and choose evil in disguise. Of precaution against this we shall have a good deal to say later, but we may note here that since the general will must naturally seek the public good, the first of all precautions is to keep it truly general. It is most general when every voter voices his own conviction, but less so when cliques and parties pledge their members all to vote as one, since there are then as many votes as there are parties only. And it practically disappears if a single party grows so powerful

---

[1] *Emile,* ii. 7.   [2] *Contrat social,* iii. 318.

as to overwhelm all others, for then there really is but one vote. So the precaution is to have small parties or none at all, and to let every man, so far as may be, vote his own opinion on the common cause—a principle well known to Solon and Lycurgus.

An act of the general will, and this alone, is law. For we have really defined law in our definition of the will itself. It will be apparent that the people only can make law, not any individual or group among them. It will also be clear that the law can deal only with the interest of all, never with any private interest, and that it must bind all alike. Nothing can be law that obligates an individual or group in any special way. Nor is it even possible for a whole people so to obligate an individual or group; for the moment they set an individual or group apart for special favour or disfavour, they are no longer the whole people, and their will no longer general. The general will must of its nature fall on all alike; and only then, only when all the people act on all the people, do we have a law.

Of course we are now speaking only of the basic or constitutional law that shapes the state. The other kinds of law, called civil or criminal, are derivatives from this and are outside our present purpose. They provide for the administration of the state, of which in due time; we are now concerned with its formation only. It is a commonplace to say that constitutional law should be impartial and above all personal consideration in shaping the state; and we are only adding that it is safely so as long as it is vested in the general will, which is of necessity impersonal. It can shape the state, and it can do no more.

It may thus create certain privileges in the state, but may not offer them to any given individuals; may make certain classes of citizens, but not admit a given citizen to any class or exclude him from it; may even order an hereditary monarchy, but not name a given man as king or family as royal. In all such matters the first act gives the state its form, while the second places individuals in it. That will come up later. Meanwhile we may now answer certain questions immemorially vexing in political philosophy. Is the king above the law? No, for he is a member of the state. Can any individual whosoever make a law? No, the common will alone can do so. Can a law be unjust? No, a people cannot be unjust to itself. It may indeed go wrong, and do itself all sorts of harm; but it cannot be tyrannical, for it cannot will its own oppression. If it seems to do that, it has ceased to rule, and something has displaced the general will. Can a people under law be free? Yes, in exact proportion to their obedience to the law. It is their own will, and whoever obeys his will is free. And we are now approaching the conclusion promised, that in surrendering our all we should inherit liberty; but of this we have still more to say.

Every state under such law is a republic, whatever its administrative form. The legitimate state is always a republic, whether it select democracy or aristocracy or monarchy as the fittest agency to execute its aims.

But how shall the people make the law? What miracle will give them, even when they are just beginning as a people, all the wisdom and the altruism necessary? And are we not assuming that, before they have a law, they will be all that the law is meant to make them?

With these questions, and to some extent still earlier, Rousseau enters on a gradual shift from the first quarter of his treatise to the portion that remains. So far he has been looking for the legitimate state in abstract reason, and reason has offered the one state that deserves the name. A union of each with all, on equal terms, for common good; with sovereignty vested in all, inalienable, indivisible; leading to law that is at one with liberty; such is the answer of reason, such the state she will produce. And so much Rousseau feels should come first. But he knows as well as any one what will threaten his ideal in practice among ordinary men, and also how the application of it must vary with a thousand exigencies of time and place. So for the rest of his treatise he is dealing more and more with applications to accord with multifarious circumstance, and with precautions to avoid violation. Most of the apparent inconsistencies within the book will disappear if this is remembered. A great deal of what he has still to say has long since passed into truism, or was such before him, and we may go lightly over most of it, omitting much entirely. Only we should note that in so doing we are disturbing the balance of his book, for he gives less space to pure abstraction than our summary would imply, and more to concrete counsel.

With a stride into the practical, for instance, Rousseau answers the questions we were asking by admitting that the people are often blind to their own good. It is all well enough to say that they cannot but desire it, and that in so far the general will must be inerrant, but often they do not and cannot know it. They need some one to show it to them, and so guard them from error and seduction. To this supremely hard task is born the lawgiver.

He is a hero if there ever was one. Modelled on men like Moses and Lycurgus, of whom Rousseau is obviously thinking, he is no less extraordinary in the unique office he is given than in the wisdom he must have to fill it. For though he must be seer enough to draft the law for the peculiar problems of his people, he must be neither sovereign to enact it nor magistrate to execute it. Either of these is fatal to his mission. He cannot be the sovereign, for we have seen that no one but the people can be that.[1] Their own will alone is binding on them, and no individual can have authority to obligate them. And we need say nothing of the practical importance of using their own will if they are to learn wisdom. But our seer must be no magistrate either if he would draft impartial law; for a magistrate continually applies the law to individuals, and cannot be expected to remain impersonal if all the while he must be personal too. Sooner or later the effect of his own law on various individuals, himself included, will sway him in the making of it. This is why Lycurgus thought it well to abdicate the kingship in order to give laws, and there are other instances in history.

So the law-giver may draft the code, but must have no power to enact it. He is only a sage who shows the people what seems wise. Be it wise or not, it becomes law only by their will; there can be no other way to make a law. And better so;

[1] He might become their *master* in two ways: either by force, which cannot be legitimate; or by agreement, which cannot change the sovereignty. The people may indeed agree to take him for their ruler and promise to obey him. Such an agreement, by which a people accept a king, was a familiar form of the social pact before Rousseau, and had often been used to justify all sorts of absolutism. Rousseau himself adopts it in the *Inequality*, but in the *Contract* he discards it as really irrelevant. If the people agree upon a ruler, they show in the very act that they are sovereign; and however they obey him, he remains an agent of their own creation. Before a people can make a pact with any ruler they must have made a pact by which they came to be a people. And that is the true Social Pact; any further contracts are administrative policies.

better even to refuse a wise law than surrender to a master of whatever wisdom. Better the chance that a people will learn wisdom under their own rule, with all their errors, than under a dictator of whatever gifts; for we know full well what the best dictators will become in due time. Our lawgiver will be none of these, but if he is worthy of his high calling he may still prevail beneficently with the people.

To the people themselves Rousseau gives three chapters, but nearly all he says has since grown so familiar as to be omissible. He is here dealing with purely practical considerations, and following Montesquieu in measuring the many influences which climate, soil, and other physical and moral circumstances must exert upon the laws of any given people. All of these the wise lawgiver will consider deeply before venturing on a constitution for his folk.

For no one constitution will be good for every people. The fundamental pact is one for every rightful state, but all that is built on it must depend on time and place and multifarious circumstance. The ideal constitution may be far from good in a given time and place. It will be durable according as it fits the circumstances and makes the most of them, but perishable if it merely carries out a principle, however excellent in the abstract, unsuitable to them.

The thing that varies with the constitution is the form of *government*. But we have hardly used this word, and we must now say what it means.

To begin with an analogy, every free act involves a will and a power to effect it. In moving to a given point, I must first decide to go there, and then my feet must take me. If either fail, I am inert. The body politic moves comparably, with a will to act and with a power to perform the action. These are called its legislative and executive functions.

The legislative function is the people's, but the executive should not be theirs. Aside from the fact that they have other things to do and cannot all be continually administering the law, and that they may therefore better trust its execution to a few of their number, we have seen that it is not well for those who make the law to execute it also. For if they are always enforcing it on individuals, they can hardly remain free from individual bias in the making of it. So they ought to leave enforcement to a minister.

That minister is the government. He may be one or many, and enjoy any title that is fitting; but he must never be confused with the sovereign, for he is its agent only. He is commissioned by the sovereign with certain powers, but the sovereign is the source of all his power, and may modify or cancel his commission at its pleasure. (And if this is common theory and practice in the modern state, we may as well remember that it was the kind of thing that got our book burned by the common hangman only a few generations since.)

The form of the government will vary as it is large or small. If the government comprises all the people, or a majority of them, it is a *democracy*;[1] if a few of them, an *aristocracy*; if one alone, a *monarchy*. But the three forms are far from absolutely fixed, for a democracy may include all of the people or only a bare majority, an aristocracy may be relatively large or small, while even monarchies have flourished with dual or plural kings or emperors; and in practice various mixed forms, as of aristocracy and monarchy, are so common as to be almost universal.

In vain the long dispute as to which of these is best. It all depends. The ideal best will not be good for every clime and people; according to conditions any one of them may be the best or worst. But in the most general terms we may say a word about the merits and defects of each.

Democracy. If those who make the law are best aware of its intention, we might argue that the government in which the people execute their law would be the perfect one. But the people will pay dearly for the privilege. The makers of the law, as we have seen, should not enforce it, or they will forget the common good for individual interest. In that path lies corruption, and it is better to risk misunderstanding than perfidy.

[1] It is important to remember that *republic* and *democracy* are not the same thing for Rousseau. A republic is a kind of state, while a democracy is only a kind of government. Any legitimate state is a republic, be it democratic, aristocratic, or monarchical in government. Democracy is the form of government in which the whole people, or a majority of them, actually wield the executive power, instead of confiding it to a few administrators. This is all a matter of definition, but we shall escape some very prevalent errors later if we remember what the definitions are. So much will be necessary, for instance, when we find Rousseau condemning democracy in favour of elective aristocracy; for what he calls elective aristocracy is virtually what we now call democracy.

And what impossible conditions would be needed for a real democracy! A state so tiny that its people could all be assembled and could all know one another, a life so simple as to cause no complicated problems or invidious dissensions, an equality in rank and fortune so exact as to make equality in right and power possible; these and many other rare conditions would be necessary. And at the best such a government would be more liable than any other to internal agitation and to civil war, and would require the greatest bravery and vigilance to live.

The truth is that there has never been a real democracy, nor ever can be. Not only is it against the order of nature that the many should govern the few, but it is out of all possibility for the people to stay constantly assembled for the public business. They can have no choice but to confide it to a commission; and the moment they do that, they have another form of government.

If there were a people of gods, they would live in a democracy, but a government so perfect is unsuitable for men.

Aristocracy. The earliest governments were aristocracies in which the heads of families held the power and their juniors ceded all authority to age; whence the words like 'priest' and 'senator' that have come down to us. In the course of time, authority was taken from the aged and given to the capable, or to those who were considered so, and thus the aristocracy became elective. Still later the authority was lodged in certain families and made hereditary; and in passing from father to son it produced occasional anomalies in senators of the ripe age of twenty.

The first or 'natural' form of aristocracy is obviously good only for a simple folk; the third, or hereditary, is the worst of all governments; while the second, or elective, is the best. It is aristocracy properly so called.[1]

It sets the government and the sovereign apart, and makes the one the agent of the other. The governors are chosen by election, or in the safest way we have invented to ensure their

[1] What Rousseau calls aristocracy is thus about the kind of government we now have in England and America, or in almost any state that we call modern.

probity and wisdom.[1] They can assemble easily and act expeditiously. And it is surely rational that the people choose a few of their best men to carry out their will rather than that they all be busy and troubled about many things which a few of them can manage better; provided always the one thing needful, that the people be the sovereign and the governors their agents only. That must be assured by all means, for the best of governments must have its imperfections, and the danger of an aristocracy is that it may ignore the general will and rule in its own name and interest.

Monarchy. The power is strongest when it lies in one hand, but the temptation to abuse it is as strong. A monarch will desire to be absolute, and so will commonly prefer a weak and unresisting people to a strong and independent one. Instead of governing the people to make them happy, he will therefore tend to make them wretched in order that he may govern them. He is likely to choose his ministers among the little men who make serviceable courtiers. If his dominion is too large for him to manage, it will suffer a lax rule, and if it is too small for his ambition, it is likely to be plunged into wars of conquest. At his death it is open to a perilous interregnum until his successor can be chosen. This is usually obviated by making the throne hereditary, but at the price of being governed at due intervals by infants, imbeciles, or monsters. Better the disturbance of elections.

And it is poor logic, however immemorial, to liken the king to the father of the state and then to clothe him with all the virtues of an ideal father by way of proving that monarchy is the best of governments. Such it might be under such a king. But to know what it will usually be in practice we must watch it under mediocre kings or bad ones—for such will commonly come to the throne, or such the throne will commonly make them.

These are the main virtues and faults of the three forms of government. In any mixed form they will make some combination corresponding to the mixture.

---

[1] But it is important to fix the method of election in the constitution; for if that is left to the government, we shall sooner or later fall back into hereditary aristocracy; the government arranging the elections to perpetuate itself. Witness the fate of Venice and other states.

Under any government the state will have its term, however, be this long or short; for any government will tend to encroach upon the sovereign, and sooner or later to usurp the sovereignty and rupture the pact. The end may come in various ways, but the destruction of the pact is the crisis in them all. A work of man's art, the state may be prolonged by a good constitution, but sooner or later it will pass, with all the works of man. If we would make it durable, we must not dream of making it eternal.

The abuse of government that follows dissolution will be *anarchy*. Specifically, democracy will turn into *ochlocracy*, aristocracy into *oligarchy*, and monarchy into *despotism*.

Among other measures to avoid these by remaining sovereign, the people should assemble for the expression of the general will at regular intervals and at other times as need arises. How the people may assemble Rousseau tries to hint in instances from ancient states in which they managed to do so, but he scarcely leaves us clear about the way they may proceed in modern nations. That is because he never finished this line of his thought. He was obviously getting ready to propose a state so small that all the people could remain the active sovereign in periodic assembly, and to provide for the protection of such small states by federation among them. So much is clear from the *Contract* itself, and clearer from the fragments since collected;[1] but the full treatment of the plan was left to the larger work which he relinquished.[2] In his view the ideal could be best approximated in small states protected from aggression through alliance.

Meanwhile he has little hope of the representative system so popular with the Parisian Anglophiles of his day. It is very like him to disapprove the idea all the more because it was in fashion, but in any case he would hardly have accepted it. If the representatives are but executives they may do well enough, and we shall have the species of elective aristocracy which we have called the best of governments. But if they usurp the sovereignty, as commonly, the state is illegitimate and the

---

[1] By Windenberger in *La République confédérative des petits états*, Paris, 1900.
[2] Cf. *Contrat social*, iii. 362, and note; *Emile*, ii. 438; and the notes to these passages in Vaughan's edition of the *Political Writings*, especially the curious story in ii. 135–6.

people are no longer free save at the moment of elections. Above all things the people must be sovereign and the government its minister.

Save for one thing we may pass over the rest of the *Contract*. The general principles remaining have all been anticipated, and the practical detail is inessential. We need not linger over matters of suffrage and elections, or trouble about the Roman comitia, the tribunate, the dictatorship, the censorship. Nothing in these will affect the idea of the state. For that matter, neither will the famous chapter on the state religion with which the treatise closes. But though clearly an afterthought, the chapter has aroused more criticism than all the rest of the book, and in particular has often been held contradictory to everything its author elsewhere utters of religion. So we must see what it says.

In the beginning every state was a species of theocracy, and there were as many gods as peoples. By the time when the Roman Empire had gathered most of the peoples into one, it had lent them all its own gods and had often borrowed theirs in turn; and in that day the known world, with a multiplicity of deities, was living under a fairly uniform cult of paganism. Then came Christianity with another empire, not of this world but of the next. But the pagans, blind to any kingdom of a world to come, fought the Christians in the conviction that the latter were only biding their time to snatch the empiry in this one. And so indeed the Christians did; no sooner did they gain the power than they made a potent despotism here below. Thus the world acquired dual rulers, Church and State, with an inevitable conflict between them; and the conflict has come down through all the centuries to our day. Though it cannot but preclude an undivided polity, all proposals for reunion of the dual rulers have so far been vain; and we are left with the strange sight of a state religion in recurrent warfare with the state itself.

The facts lead men like Bayle to argue that any religion is an evil for the state, and others like Warburton to reply that any state will find its best support in Christianity. Both the arguments would seem to be wrong. For history seems rather to show that any state will need a religion to make its people love their duty, but also that the Christian faith has done more harm than good in purely civil polity. And it is of such polity alone, of course, that we are speaking—of what may help the state to endure in harmony. Not the truth or error of any creed is now in question, but its import only to the civil order.

In that aspect there are two kinds of religion. One is a religion without rites or temples, dwelling only in the heart of man; such the pure faith of the Gospels or the true theism. This is a natural religion and could be a universal one, for it is justified of sentiment and reason to all men alike. By virtue of that very fact it cannot be a state religion, for it will not stop with any territorial boundary. It cannot belong to a single people if it holds for all the world. The other is a state religion pure and simple. Fixed and prescribed for a peculiar people, it is not only in the state's control but is literally one with the state; and it ceases at the national boundary, beyond which all is infidelity. Such is the tribal religion of a primitive folk; such, for instance, the creed of Moses.

Out of these two we have made a mixture that is stranger but now commoner than either. It is neither national nor universal. It is not universal because it is prescribed within a given state or states; but it is not truly national because it is a separate power in the state and often at strife with it. Such is the religion of the Lamas or the Japanese, and such is Roman Christianity.

For the civil order there is danger in all three religions. In the last it is too obvious for comment. There can be no good polity in giving man two laws, two rulers, and two incompatible duties; that is but the way to people all the world with Guelfs and Ghibellines. In the tribal religion, love of the gods and love of country are one and the same, with obvious advantages in polity; but at the price of credulity, intolerance, and bloodshed. For as long as a people feel it holy to fight others for the glory of their gods, they will live in a state of war precarious to civil order.

There is left the pure faith of the Gospels. To that sublime ideal of the union of all men as brothers even beyond death we shall elsewhere offer our devotion.[1] But if we must now

---

[1] In the *Savoyard Vicar's Profession*, as discussed in the next chapter.

ask of its influence in the civil order, we shall find some inconvenience in it. If it is real, it will be indifferent to the states of this world, and will even detach us from them, as from all things here below; and instead of being the main sanction of the law and of the civil bond, it will become an agency of dissolution. To the true Christian nothing matters in this vale of tears. States may come and states may go, battles may be lost or won, and tyrants may oppress and torture; let him be but pure in heart, and all will be well with him in a little while, his very resignation to the present evil making his reward to come the surer. If the danger appear fanciful, it is only because there are so few real Christians; but we are speaking now of such alone, having just considered other kinds. And we are forced to think that a republic of true Christians, however meek, however just and virtuous, would not long endure.

If we are still convinced that any state will be the better with a religion at its basis, what is left? In answering we may turn back once more to the pact with which we started. Under it the sovereign was supreme in all that mattered to the common good, the individual free in all else; and we must now apply the principle even to religious faith. For it matters greatly to the common weal that every individual have a faith which will inspire love of civic duty, and so much the sovereign may require of any one who wants to be a member of the state; but the sovereign can have no interest in the individual's faith except as it affects his social duty, and beyond that he is free to believe as he will.

There will therefore be a purely civil faith, and the sovereign will lay down its articles; but less as a religious creed than as a civic sentiment and duty. No one will be forced to embrace it, but any one who cannot do so may be excluded from the state—not because he is an infidel, but only because he is lacking in the necessary civic spirit. We have already spoken of the high development of public spirit that Rousseau requires in the citizen, and we have now to add that he is sure it cannot flower without the inspiration of religion. That is why he holds to a religion for the state. It is why he proposes the worst of all punishments for any man who lies about the faith. For any man who shall embrace it with a lie, and prove his own hypocrisy in daily conduct, may be put to death—not as an unbeliever, but as the worst of all civil offenders, as a traitor.[1]

The dogmas of the civil religion will be few and simple, but precise: the existence of God, the future life of man, the happiness of the good, the punishment of the wicked, and the sanctity of the social pact and of the law. These for affirmations; for all prohibition we may be content to disallow intolerance. We may permit any further belief in the individual which is consonant with these and tolerant of all. But whoso shall be so intolerant as to say that there is no salvation except in his own faith is too unsociable to be a citizen and shall be separated from the state.

[1] This is the cause of the recrimination. It is possibly the classic case of inconsistency in all Rousseau; and what is to be said of it will apply with due allowance to nearly all the other cases. In every other place, and above all in the Vicar's *Profession*, Rousseau is an ardent advocate of religious tolerance; in the one passage on the state religion he prescribes the penalty of death for recreants. If the contradiction is as great as it has often seemed, there is only one thing to say of it: that at every other point Rousseau is in search of a religion to convince the individual, but that here alone he is intent on a religion to sustain the state; and that he does not find the two entirely identical. If his reasoning is unsatisfactory, since a faith that will perpetuate the state must surely be convincing to its members, it is all too reminiscent of the trouble other men have had in framing one ideal for the state and individual alike; and we have made it clear that Rousseau is prone enough to follow logic to its limits on the problem immediately before him. Even so, the explanation is not very plausible. The *Social Contract* and *Emile*, with the Vicar's *Profession* in it, were written at the same time; they were not only published together, but are so interpenetrated that the first is reproduced all but entire within the second; and it is next to impossible that, on the very subject of religion which occupied the author more than any other, they would be left in glaring contradiction. So we had better see just how great the contradiction is. The Vicar believes in his religion because it does not seem individual to him, but, in reason, universal; yet he would tolerate all other religions which are tolerant in turn, condemning only those which hold that we are damned if we do not believe them. Having no power to prohibit such intolerance, he can only do his best to discourage it. Meanwhile, as a member of the state, he devoutly follows its religious ordinances. The *Contract* offers a religion to support the state. Its dogmas are about identical with those of the Vicar; but any further dogmas will be tolerated in the individual unless they are themselves intolerant—unless they say we shall be damned for not believing them. If they do, the state may do more than discourage them, it may prohibit them; and whoso holds them may therefore be excluded from the state as unfit for membership. So the contradiction looks like a pretty fair agreement. Of course the man who tries to get the better of the state by lying about his religion pays a dearer penalty than most of us would now approve. But we may object to it on almost any other ground than that of inconsistency. The man is not put to death for his religion, or his lack of it, but for a lie about the most important of all things for the state, about his submission to the sovereign. He is executed as a traitor. We may wish his sentence were less harsh, but its very rigour is an instance of consistency; it shows above all things how much Rousseau meant when he spoke of surrendering our all to the supreme authority of the general will. Such consistency may possibly be worse than inconsistency, but it cannot well be both.

A society of free consent, and not of force; a union of each with all on equal terms for common good; a sovereignty vested in all and voiced by the general will for the maintenance of liberty in law : this is the heart of the *Social Contract*. All else, whether repeated or omitted here, is contingent, variable, precautionary. So much is the absolute necessity for the right state; or since it is derived in reason from the very nature of our species, for the natural society.

II

Surely politics must be the desperate science. Alone in his ivory tower, the sage who sketches an ideal state may well have the hardest of all human enterprises; when he looks down at an actual people seething in ignorance and prejudice and mob hysteria, he must often shrink in dismay from what they will do with his dream when it is delivered to their mercies. Yet there is unusual comfort in the fact that, with all our errors and misunderstandings, we have come much nearer the ideal just reviewed than were the peoples who first read it only a few generations since; so much nearer that we need an effort of imagination to remember the appalling political conditions in which it arose.

To omit all desolate detail, we may say at once that hardly any people of the modern world would seem to have gone farther than the men around Rousseau from the government by the consent of the governed which he has here been advocating and which nearly all of us have since accepted as the first essential of legitimacy in the state. Hardly any modern people would seem to have known a tyranny more absolute in its oppugnancy to right and reason. And though the better thought in politics was sounder than the wretched government in power, it was still a very tangled skein. Centuries of political philosophy had left many men still wondering whether the very evils they were all but unendurably abiding were not the inevitable product of the 'natural law'; whether the prince who made all laws could in turn be subject to any; whether a king, even a Louis, had not been anointed by divine right as the direct deputy of a God of lovingkindness; as whether the right of the strongest, the institution of slavery, and many other things now felt to be as noxious in reason as in practice, were not necessary in the order of nature and commanded from on high. There were better notions in the air, of course, and all of them of ancient lineage, but these were still among the stock in trade of the political philosopher. To such passes had the intellect of man been brought in trying to reason out how we should dwell in amity together.

Such mists evaporate before a work like the *Social Contract*. The rule of a Louis is simply illegitimate, the right of the strongest is a mere contradiction in terms; the prince who makes the law is a pure fiction if no prince or other man can make a law, and the notion of divine right has no meaning for a people that is sovereign. And similarly with a score of other problems. Not for a moment need this imply that the *Contract* alone put them out of court. Nearly all of it was in the air before, and often very long before; and Rousseau is in debt to many predecessors. But if his borrowings are evident—though it may be hard to state them precisely because he pondered them so long in reverie that they reached a form rather peculiarly his own—the fusion that he made of them still keeps its place as the most original utterance in political philosophy from his century.[1]

For a single illustration we may take the very idea of the social pact. The notion that society begins with some kind of contract had come down all the way from the Middle Ages and even has an ancestry in Greece. By Rousseau's time it was such a truism in political philosophy that a treatise on the state without it would have been rather like a modern essay in biology without the evolutionary theory. The very title of the *Social Contract* is the most conventional name that could have been found for it. For all that, the meaning of the pact is rather different in Rousseau from what it is in any of his predecessors, even in Locke—possibly about as different as the evolutionary theory in a modern scientist and in Darwin.

[1] He probably owes most to Plato, Hobbes, Locke above all, and Montesquieu, in spite of many differences from each of them and of a fundamental conflict with Hobbes in particular; while he names about a dozen other predecessors, and may owe something to still others whom he does not mention. But it is neither possible nor very useful to say precisely where he found all his ideas; asking where an eighteenth-century thinker heard about the social pact or the general will is rather like asking where one of us heard of constitutional government.

Prior to Rousseau the pact had commonly been treated, though not always, as a thing of the dim past—as a contract made in prehistoric days to form the first society. There are lingerings of the notion in Rousseau as well, but only linger-ings. His pact is an agreement we must make now if we are to have the right society; there is nothing else in reason upon which to found one. The point is not unimportant. For the misprision into which the whole idea of the social pact has now fallen seems to rest all but entirely on contempt for any notion that a pact was ever drawn up in the dawn of history by certain savages in solemn conference to institute a state. Of course that notion is preposterous. But if the pact be taken as a tacit or express agreement made among the members of a free state and more or less reiterated in a thousand simple acts like voting or acknowledging the rule of the majority, it is not so easy to dismiss from reason.

Prior to Rousseau the pact had often varied with the people making it. Almost any species of agreement that would satisfy their fancy might become their social pact, and there might be about as many pacts as there were peoples. For Rousseau there is but one. It does not depend upon the fancy of the people making it, but upon the nature of the case that brings them to it; and as the case is everywhere the same, so is the pact. It is no more possible to think of various kinds of pact than of various kinds of rectitude.

Prior to Rousseau the pact had often been either (a) a simple contract of the people with a ruler, he to command and they to obey; or (b) a dual contract, first among the people to set up a state, and then between them and a ruler to command it. So the contract with the ruler had commonly been either the entire pact or a good part of it; often much the greater part. There is nothing more important in our author's treatise than the act by which he wipes out the contract with the ruler and leaves that among the people as the only social pact. In so doing he makes the people the sole sovereign, and any government their agent only; in a word, he lays down the first principle of what we now call a democracy.

Under the one true pact he argues that the law will terminate the age-old conflict between state and individual by giving to the one an incontestable authority and to the other an inviolable liberty. That belief remains for further scrutiny. But we may say in passing that these ideas of the pact, although no one of them is absolutely novel, form a combination that may claim a fair originality.[1] They are the heart of his political theory; and their consonance with one another and with his more general doctrine may appear as we proceed with his idea that true law and liberty are one.

Either the state is made for man or it is purposeless. The test of its sufficiency must therefore be its fitness to his nature. As with every other question in our author, we are back at this beginning.

From the Roman jurists down it had been customary to begin a treatise of society with a picture of the 'state of nature' antecedent to it and a list of correspondent 'natural rights' with which it had to reckon. That more or less supposititious state of nature had been painted in all hues. The century before Rousseau had left two main descriptions of it, but in hopeless contrast. Hobbes had filled it with a set of brutes in constant war of all with all, and Locke had peopled it with a company of Christian gentlemen long before their time—or with just about the kind of natural heroes that Rousseau is popularly thought to have believed in. But Rousseau's state of nature is a sort of mean between the two. It is peopled by mere human animals who have no more reason for perpetual war than those of any other species, and who own indeed a certain sympathy or social instinct that makes them do more good than harm, upon the whole, to one another, but who enjoy no greater bliss than these facts would imply.

Aside from the *Inequality*, however, where there is a special reason for it, Rousseau does not make much of the state of nature or of any natural rights inviolable in us simply because we may have owned them when we lived in such a state. He bases his society upon our nature, in all earnest, for other basis he knows none; but our nature is not something we enjoyed long ago in brutehood and lost on the way up into polity. It is

[1] As has often been noted; perhaps best by Beaulavon, whose *Introduction* to the *Contrat social* is a modest classic to which these pages are frequently indebted (2nd edition, Paris, 1914).

rather the thing we cannot lose; the thing that is essential to us now and always, or without which we could never have endured and cannot in reason be conceived. What Rousseau thinks this thing to be we have already said.[1] We have also said that the most important point about it is that it is capable of indefinite development in good or evil, and we have given Rousseau's test for good and evil in its growth. Just as the right education is one means to its proper growth, the right society is another; and the two in harmony will speed our ascent toward the fulfilment of our nature. Now if there be any such thing as a natural right, it will be something that is necessary to that ascent. It is not a right because we may have had it when we were all brutes, for that is no sort of credential, but because we have to have it in order to rise above the brute.

We cannot rise without some sort of freedom. Under bondage we could make no choice of our path. So freedom of some kind is a necessity that we may call a natural right.

But we have seen that there are several kinds of freedom. In the state of nature, if there ever was one, we enjoyed the kind that we call simple independence. We were limited by our own powers, by any arbitrary interference from our fellows or from other creatures, and by all the forces of the world of matter, but otherwise we did exactly as we pleased. Our independence was the lowest form of freedom known— the freedom of the brute to be the creature of desire. In a society some of it will vanish. As soon as there are rules allowing certain actions and forbidding others, we must lose the privilege of doing as we please. If the rules are made by one of us, or by a few, and forced on all the others, we have quit our independence and entered into something comparable to slavery. If they are agreed upon by all of us and willingly obeyed by every one, we have risen out of independence into civil liberty—the only kind of liberty that we shall mean when we employ the word. For liberty is about as different from independence on the one hand as from slavery on the other. Independence consists in doing as we please, and slavery in doing as another pleases; but liberty in doing as we all agree to do. What we all agree upon becomes our *right*, and the word

[1] *Ante*, pp. 12 ff.

can have no meaning except as we agree upon it. Security in rights is what we mean by the form of freedom we are calling liberty.[1]

So we must give up something to inherit liberty; and if we are to have it we may first make sure of what we must surrender as the price of it. We must surely yield a portion of our independence, and a little thought will show us that we have to yield it all. For if we ask what reason we can have for giving up a kind of freedom in order to have a society, we can only answer that we want the power of a group to help us toward our ends—to speed us in the ascent we are making. Yet we have seen that for the ascent we shall want a kind of freedom still. And if we fuse the two desires, we shall find that we are asking for a society which has full power and yet allows full liberty— that we really want the strongest power we can have behind us and the greatest liberty compatible before us. For Rousseau there is one society alone that answers the two aims—the one that rises on the Social Pact and remains true to it. The power will certainly be strong just in proportion as we give up individual independence to create a common force, and strongest when we give up all of it; so we shall get the most if 'each of us gives his person and his total power to the common cause'. That is the price we pay. And it remains for Rousseau to show that if we pay that price to the 'supreme authority of the general will' we shall come into the fullest liberty that can be known to us. If he can do that, he will have proved that the pact we are repeating is no arbitrary fancy, but the simple requisite of reason for the state; or that the first necessity for liberty is the surrender of our all before the law.

It may be said in passing that there are other reasons why the surrender must be total. We may as well admit that there are no natural rights so imprescriptible that no society may take them from us, for they are literally unthinkable; there are no such things as rights except as a society creates them. If we try to reserve vague portions of our pristine independence, we can have no guaranty for them, for the society cannot confirm

[1] And we have said that the discipline of civil liberty may lead to that highest form of freedom known as moral liberty; but this belongs to ethics and need not be treated here. Cf. *ante*, pp. 28 ff.

what has never come within its ken. If we still reserve our several portions, we shall start unequal, and we have seen in the *Inequality* how the disparities will swell to mammoth size under the social order. Still worse, none of us will know exactly what he has surrendered or reserved, or where the power of the state begins and ends; and we shall be for ever struggling to retain the most against a sovereign striving to exact the most, with a resultant clash between the individual and the law, or jumble of the state of nature and the civil order, which is the worst of polities. And in truth there is hardly such a thing as partial surrender to the law. If it means obeying when I like and disobeying when I can, it is no sort of obedience, but the mere indulgence of desire; it is simple anarchy, or the state of nature all over again. If it means obeying only when I must, it is no obedience still, but a surrender to mere force; the state is illegitimate and there is no law in it, but only the edict of a master. For all these reasons it is evident that any one who wants to make a partial surrender, and so try to live in a jumble of the state of nature and the civil order, cannot well know what it is he wants. 'Always at strife within himself, always bandied between duty and desire, he will be neither man nor citizen.'[1] The one thing rational is complete surrender in equality before the law.

But I was to be free, and now I am surrendering my all! Where is the liberty the state will give me? The question comes to any reader at this point; it has troubled many a philosopher and embittered many a page of criticism. And it marks the crisis of our theory, for by the answer to it the main argument will stand or fall. The answer is possibly the most original idea in the book before us, and certainly the hardest to interpret; and for that reason we may do well to state it first, all paradoxical as it may sound, and to explain it afterward. The answer is that law can have no power to abridge our liberty.

We shall know what this means when we know what law is. First of all, we must get rid of any notion that it is the edict of a man or of a group of men compelling us to act against our will. No such thing is law, but only force. Law is not made by compulsion, but by agreement. It is the voice of the general

[1] *Emile*, ii. 7.

will, and never anything but that. It therefore has the following character:

1. It deals only with the common cause. No man will care about a thing of no concern to him, nor a community about a matter that can have no interest for it. So the law is limited at once to corporate affairs, and in the sphere of private interest I am free. Not because I am still clinging to the shreds of my old independence am I free there, nor even because the law has taken pains to certify my freedom, but simply because no law can of its nature trouble with my private interest. An individual ruler may indeed invade it for his own advantage, but the common will can never do so. If such a thing occurs, it is not the common will that is at work. So I am free in all my personal affairs by virtue of no alterable human ordinance, but by the very nature of the law.

2. It is made by all alike. I have just the same share as all others in the making of it. But a share in its creation must imply a promise to obey it when it is created. Unless I make such a promise, no one needs to make it; and we shall have the mad sight of a law that no one offers to obey. In entering my vote I thus consent to all the law that may come from the voting, for there are no other terms in which a vote has meaning. But I so consent because I so desire. My supreme wish for the state is that it may live in law, and I offer my consent because there else can be no law. So in offering it and living up to it I am fulfilling my chief aim, or doing what I most desire to do; and doing what I most desire is liberty.

3. It is binding upon all alike. When I vote, I obligate myself in common with all others, as do they; and no one of us can lay a burden on another which he is not willing to endure in his own part. It is therefore inconceivable that we shall vote for tyranny. No one can want a tyranny unless he is himself above it; no one but an individual ruler can desire it. So there can be no tyranny in law; and where there is no tyranny, there is liberty.

4. It is made for the common good. If I have so far been thinking as an individual of what the law will do for me, I must now hasten as a citizen to consider all that I must do if I would have a law. So long as I vote only for the most that it can give me, I am in no state to gain the most it has to offer. I have seen

that law deals only with the common cause, and lets my private interest alone; but it can treat the common cause, as I must realize, only in so far as I and all my fellows sink our private interests in the act of its creation and espouse the public good. Unless we can do so much for the sake of law, we shall never have one; we shall never voice the general will which is its sole creator. Only in the measure that we do so are we citizens, and in so far as we come short we are still individuals lingering in the state of nature and lusting for the fleshpots of our former independence. We are not fit for liberty. But in so far as we forget our personal interest in the making of the law, we shall secure the kind of law that has been shown to keep us free. If we can but remember this, we shall need no miracle of altruism to live up to it, but only common sense enough to seek our greatest good. And we cannot be more free than in the liberty to seek our highest good.

Such is the character of law. Because it must of nature leave us free in any personal matter, because it must fulfil our chief desire for the corporate concern, and because it cannot suffer tyranny, the law will have no way to tamper with our liberty, but will be the single warrant for it. The reason why it has taken so much time for us to find this out is only that we have so long given the name of law to things that have no title to it. But the decrees of arbitrary rulers, which may certainly abolish liberty, are no longer law for us. They will be unknown in our state. We alone can make the law that will keep us free.

But when I am outvoted and subjected to a law I do not like, am I still at liberty? Assuredly. I never dreamed that liberty meant having my own way in all things. If I ever had that in the ancient state of nature, I was glad to give it up for something better; and if I know what I am saying I shall not begin to prate about a loss of liberty because the better thing turns out to be a little different from having all my own way. I knew well enough it would be different. I renounced my own sweet way in order to become a member of the sovereign that should make the law. In so doing I consented to the law that should be made—not to certain portions of it that might please me, but to all of it. A fine consent it would have been if I had offered to obey the law in case it suited me! In other words, I knew that the sovereign would seldom be unanimous and that the rule of the majority would be the only way in which the general will could work. I understood the rule of the majority to be inherent in the pact, and I consented to it at the start. In this way all the laws it makes go back to the unanimity of the pact empowering it to make them. But I know as well that the majority rules over me, not by virtue of its numbers or its force, for these could make no right, but only by virtue of my own consent to its authority.

The consent was necessary to the law, and my main desire as a civil being is a reign of law. I can have it only as I honour my consent; and to have my main desire, I need hardly say again, is liberty. For the main desire I may well have to forego a minor one. That is a condition even of my individual life; for I may often have more than one desire, and renounce a lesser for a greater, with no sense of losing liberty thereby. It is likewise a condition of all civil life, and with no greater loss. In both realms I choose the greater and renounce the less. That is what occurs whenever I obey a law I do not like in order that there may be law. Only when I renounce the greater for the less do I lose liberty by going counter to my main desire. And that is what occurs whenever I break a law. Even if I feel a specious sense of freedom in so doing, it is only because I have forgotten that I am also breaking the more fundamental law which it is my highest wish to keep. I interrupt the reign of law to satisfy a whim, and in so defeating a great end for a little one I lose in liberty. What I have really done is to reach back for a morsel of the ancient independence I was fain to give up. And that, once more, is why it was so necessary for me to give up every bit of it. Only as I do so shall I have a law; but if I can really do so, the law cannot abridge my liberty.

When we really know that the evasion of the law is bondage, and that only our 'obedience to the law that we have made is liberty',[1] we shall be fit members for the state. We need not dream that it is easy to be fit—to leave the individual behind and enter on the common life. We have not implied that liberty is facile of inheritance, for it is the end of all our striving. Independence is far easier; as much so as the evasion of a law we do

[1] *Contrat social,* iii. 316.

not like is easier than obedience to it. We shall be fit in such measure as we can remember that evasion merely multiplies our bonds, and that lawlessness alone, not law, will rob us of our freedom. In the most familiar parlance, every lawless act is wrong because it tends to nullify the constitution which is the bulwark of our liberty. All of which may make it hard to say whether the most striking thing about our author's famous theory of law is the subtlety that has entangled many a critic or the simplicity that has made it the first axiom of the modern state.

The perfect unison of law and liberty may finally receive ideal illustration from an item in our educational theory that is equally in point here. We have said that man is subject to two kinds of limitation for which we employ the single name of law —to the law of matter and the law of men. His dependence on the law of earth and air is all but unperceived, for it is not in his nature to rebel thereat; but his dependence upon that of men is often irritating, for he cannot but resent their interference. The inference in education was that we should govern children by no proclamation of our will above their own, but by keeping it in sure and silent operation like a natural force. The comparable inference for the state is that the law should reign, not like the arbitrary will of one man on another, but like the impartial and irrevocable laws of nature; and in so far as this may be, we shall obey the law of men as we obey the laws of earth and air, with no sense of limitation and with hardly any even of obedience. 'If the law of man could only be, like that of nature, so irrevocable that no human force could break it, our dependence on our kind would be like our dependence on the world of matter, and our society would then combine all the advantage of the state of nature with that of the civil state.[1]' There would be many things we could not do, but we should not dream of trying them, for we should not even want to do them. Such law that we should have if ever we were perfect citizens, and such the liberty.

[1] *Emile*, ii. 52.

III

That the state described was far to seek in Rousseau's day is very evident. The governments in power were proceeding mainly on a very different principle, and that is why the *Inequality* was written to deplore them. That the state is still beyond us is but too apparent. Even that it will remain somewhat beyond us for all time might go unsaid but for the fact that many of the critics seem to start and end with the idea that Rousseau thought it could be instituted at a human nod. It is frankly an ideal, though it has already had a large effect in practice, and the only question left for us is whether the ideal is a good one. What has been objected to it?

That it is abusable is evident enough. Of course a demagogue may counterfeit a public spirit for his personal ends, and so may any group. Of course a busybody may forget the common cause to meddle in his neighbour's private business. Of course it takes a certain wisdom to be citizen enough to know that obedience to the law is liberty, and a certain prudence to act consonantly. The ideal has been grievously abused, whether by men who understood its meaning or by others who were ignorant of it. Rousseau foresaw a thousand ways of injuring law and liberty in the betrayal of his principle, and was decidedly uncomfortable about what he well knew to be the desperate science. So apprehensive was he as to say outright that few peoples were intelligent and public-spirited enough to compass liberty, and that for the rest some other polity were better;[1] so apprehensive that he filled a good half of his book with precautions against error; and indeed so apprehensive that in spite of an occasional hope of adapting the ideal to some people like the Poles or Corsicans, his more usual mood was one of a despair perhaps too deep lest it could never be approximated in human society, and lest the most arbitrary despotism, the most 'perfect Hobbism', should prove the only possible alternative.[2] For he was sure the sovereign must be absolute if the state would live; and if the sovereign could not be the people, it would have to be a master. He never doubted the

---

[1] *Contrat social*, iii. 330.
[2] *Lettre à Mirabeau*; Vaughan, *Political Writings*, ii. 161.

ideal, but he often wondered how far it could go in practice. Yet he thought best to state it once for all, and let it work as it could. Whatever its worth, it may be no more abusable than any other social principle. And a principle is not invalidated by abuses merely, else the golden rule would be the most discredited of maxims.

It is hard to say whether the *Contract* has been oftener indicted for an individualism that will run to anarchy or for an absolutism that will bring the final tyranny. The people rule, and may do as they please; the people is supreme, and its pleasure will be despotism; so run the unsisterly opinions. On the whole, the first is older and more popular, the second later and more learned; but the two have come from every decade and from every kind of critic, and have even found a common home in season with a single critic. Vaughan can see them both implicit in the marvellous diatribes of Burke which are probably the main source of the Anglo-Saxon creed about our book. In 1790 Burke is aghast at the men who are disbanding France into her original *moleculae*, or murdering a nation to give every man his own sweet will. But six years later he is in a rage because individuality is left out of their scheme and the state is all in all for them; because they are surrendering the last morsel of their liberty for a sop to Leviathan. Of course Burke is speaking of two sets of revolutionists, with the Terror and much else between them, and apart from the intemperate eloquence of age he may be mainly right about them both; but he cannot well be right in implying or openly declaring that they are both doing the will of Rousseau. Yet in some sort of amity the two opinions have come down the century to us, now in diatribe and now in eulogy, and are still assuring us on the one hand that our treatise is a charter for individual licence and on the other that it 'leaves no jot of liberty' to any individual, but is 'one of the most potent implements of tyranny that maniac ever forged.'[1]

Though famous in their sponsors, the opinions cannot both be right unless our treatise is a tissue of such incoherence as to merit no attention. But without answering that it is also assailed by Burke and others for a logic which they call too

[1] Lemaître, *Jean-Jacques Rousseau*, pp. 259, 267.

unrelenting, we may simply ask if there is anything of signal incoherence in the summary as given of it. In the light of such a summary both opinions seem to be untenable. The book is meant for neither individualist nor absolutist. In the struggle between state and individual which has been the torment of political philosophy from Aristotle down, it offers a proposal for a peace. Whatever the proposal may be worth, we have already stated it so fully that we may now be brief upon it. The individual must have liberty for progress, but the state that fosters progress must have power to do its work. The liberty must be secure, for a precarious liberty is none at all, but the power must be supreme, for contingent power is the lack of it. So the two must remain full and unconflicting. And our author would so render them in law that cannot of its nature lack supremacy but cannot of its nature limit liberty. The reasoning that leads him to such law may be assailed in other ways—as a sheer abstraction, as ideal or 'metaphysical' perhaps; but not as individualist or absolutist.

For it is such reasoning that arouses what has nearly always been the main objection to the book, especially in lands that speak the tongue of Burke. The whole thing is airy logic—logic soaring in a void above the reach of fact or care of consequence. The age of sophisters has come indeed, with Rousseau as the worst and loudest of them, and 'the glory of Europe is extinguished for ever' with a libertine logician fiddling on the thin strings of intellectual figment in the ruins.[1] Morley carries on the charge more temperately than most of its continuators, and in periods so masterly that we may borrow all our illustrations from him. Over and over he tells us that many of the problems in our treatise are such pure dialectic as 'never had any other than an abstract and phantasmatic existence', and that 'the slightest attempt to confront them with actual fact would have shown them to be not merely valueless, but meaningless'. A 'symmetrical' humour made Rousseau's ' vision too narrow' for his complex subject, and led only to his 'geometrical method' of handling the kind of 'desperate absurdity' that makes 'fanatics'. Many of his pages are mere 'logical deductions from verbal definitions' that lead only to

[1] Rivington ed., 1803, v. 149.

questions which 'were never worth asking' and to answers which 'nobody will take the trouble to deny' because they are 'nonsense'. For though he is 'firmly possessed with the infallibility of his own dreams', he is merely 'basing his political institutions on a figment', as if he 'had never really settled the ends for which government exists;' so he can give us 'not the least help toward the solution of any problem of actual government'. Never mind if he is nothing but a sentimentalist still, who offers mere 'emotion for the discovery of law', for all his logic is the fig-leaf of his sentiment. And never mind if Morley, after reassuring us in closing that he is innocent of all 'attempt to palliate either the shallowness or the practical mischievousness' of the book, gives us a last surprise by showing how it fired thousands of 'generous breasts' all over Europe to a 'virile and patriotic energy' so great as to create a new social world which reminds Morley of the new world of science after Newton. Such a surprise is very common for the reader of the criticism of Rousseau. But Rousseau, of all men, must not have the credit; he did but 'involuntarily and unconsciously contribute to the growth of those new and progressive ideas, in which for his own part he lacked all faith'—even though he was 'firmly possessed with the infallibility' of them.[1]

All this from a famous liberal known for moderation, all this from a single chapter of the best book in the language on our subject. We would not be unfair to its author, nor could he have so understood us; for the opinions we have quoted from his early masterpiece deepened steadily within him during the half-century of service that ensued upon their utterance. If we were looking for excitement we could fill a hundred pages with quotations from as many authors whose intemperance would leave the present excerpts rather pale. But these should be enough to serve the purpose.

There is no denying that there is a truth behind them. Every reader of the *Social Contract* must have felt it. There is more abstraction in the book than practical experience, and at cardinal points. 'It is as if the edifice were built of wood instead of human beings, so precisely are the pieces fitted into place by

[1] All the quotations are from the chapter on the *Social Contract* in Morley's *Rousseau*.

rule and line.' Slip this into Burke or Morley, and the words
will fit to all perfection; but it is not Burke or Morley now pro-
testing—it is no other than Rousseau in person. Such is
Emile's first objection to the *Social Contract* as abridged for
his instruction. And his tutor has an answer ready. 'True,' he
says, 'but we must remember that the right is not dependent
upon human passion, and that our first duty was to settle the
true principle of social right. Now that we have found it, we
may look and see what men have made of it, *et vous verrez de
belles choses!*'[1] So Rousseau knew at least what he was doing
when he built his doctrine mainly out of logic. If his admission
lay obscure in some far corner of his work, a critic might be
more excusable for missing it and for implying that Rousseau
never thought of it and never dreamed of any other key to
social theory than that of formal logic; but time and again the
admission is explicit, and by implication it is omnipresent. It
is clear, for instance, in his reference to Montesquieu, so famous
for another way in social theory. 'The illustrious Montesquieu'
is the only man who could have found the true principle of
social right, 'but he took care to avoid the principles of politics
and gave all his attention to the laws of actual governments;
and the two matters are as different as may be. But whoever
would pass judgement on an actual government must study
both of them; he must know what ought to be if he would
judge what is.'[2]

Rousseau's quest is mainly for what ought to be, and Montesquieu's for what has been and is. The one would find the
right first and apply it as may be expedient, and the other looks
for the expedient in the faith that nothing else is right. It is
no disrespect to either to say this. It is fortunate enough that
neither tried to be the other; as fortunate, in a minor way, as
that a Plato did not try to be an Aristotle, or, in a more comparable instance, as that Edmund Burke would seldom follow
abstract reason very far on any of the principles which it was
his sovereign principle to flout. But we do not escape principles
by flouting them, we only assert others; and if Burke had ever
deigned to justify his sovereign principle in final reason, he
might have had his troubles. Rousseau had his own in follow-

[1] *Emile*, ii. 439. [2] *Ibid.* 430.

ing Montesquieu in the details of practical experience; partly because he found so little room for rivalry, mainly because he was not made for sifting masses of detail but rather for carving out a principle. So he is weakest in the latter portion of his book, where observation and experience count for most; he is weakest in 'examples', here as in *Emile*. He is stronger in the earlier portion, where he must rely on reason pure and simple. In that reliance he will find a single right society, as did Plato long before him on the same ground—on the ground that there can be one kind of justice only. On the ground of observation and experience, Montesquieu will hold a single right society to be pure fiction.

These are the two ways for the political philosopher. He may gather all the facts of variable experience in the hope that he may then deduce a principle from them, even though it prove that any principle is inconceivable. Such is on the whole the way of Montesquieu or Burke. Or he may first look for a principle in reason, in the hope that he may mould the facts in some proportion to its image. Such is on the whole the way of Plato or Rousseau. On the whole, of course; it would be tedious to show that we must use some combination of the two, since the purest reason must have facts to go on, and since we cannot even gather facts without some reason for so doing. We must 'study both'. We are all using both the methods all the time, and they often yield about the same results in practice, as they did indeed for Montesquieu and Rousseau; for in practical conclusions about government the two men are pretty much at one. There is little ground for any man who may prefer one method to revile his neighbour for employing the other; and when the results are similar, the men will be left fighting over nothing but their badges. There would probably have been no better magistrate for Rousseau's commonwealth than Burke, for all his eloquent derision of its author.

Now Rousseau does not so much choose between the two ways as endorse them both but try to show that one of them must take precedence. Though he was one of the earliest men of genius to offer ample praise to the great Montesquieu, he still thought that the study of what ought to be must come first, else the study of what is, however thorough, could not know its purpose. He was sure the endless gathering of facts was useless in the absence of a principle to judge them by. And he was sure the principle must come from reason, for he saw no hope of its emerging by some spontaneity from the facts alone; as well hope that the golden rule will rise out of a list of all our deeds as that the golden age will be discoverable in the facts of our history.[1] That is why he wove the *Social Contract* mainly out of logic. In our Darwinian day the other method has the upper hand, in social science as in all else; in the still Cartesian day of Rousseau, his own way was in far higher favour. The century was out for universals, in spite of Montesquieu, and Rousseau was of it. For whatever be the common notion, he probably owes more in general method to Descartes than to any other predecessor, and the *Social Contract* may well be the best example of Cartesian reasoning since Descartes himself.

But reasoning it is, of full intention; and that is what has caused most of the criticism. For the main target of the scorn of Burke and Morley is simply the use of reason as such in a realm where they believe it to be unemployable and pernicious. Nor is their belief at all unusual. Many a man considers that our safest policy is to feel our way from point to point as best we can, rather than to map out a complete itinerary at the start and try to cling to it. But there need be no derision for the other men who think that we must know where we are going if we are to find the way. And such men may say that cavilling at reason as such in any realm is a little too much like cavilling at the *Republic*, a favourite adolescent pastime, because it is not 'practical', or even at Euclid because there are no straight lines in nature, or at any abstract thought at all because there is nothing but brute fact before our eyes. The mind's eye has another vision, which alone may better the brute fact around us. Undoubtedly the vision may be wrong, and dangerous.

[1] The most unfortunate way in which he ever said this is in the famous epigram, so often misinterpreted and ridiculed, in the *Discourse on Inequality* (i. 83): 'Let us lay aside all the facts, for they have no bearing on our problem.' It is true that the *facts* in question are those in the first chapter of Genesis, and that Rousseau is avoiding the inquisitors with a time-honoured formula (Let us suppose there were no Bible, what would reason tell us?); but he is skilful enough to put two meanings in one phrase, not foolish enough to think that knowledge grows with ignorance of fact, which is a common misinterpretation of the passage.

Undoubtedly it may be misinterpreted, and made more dangerous. We have said that reason is a perilous weapon in our hands. We are always busy sweeping its past wrecks away, and we should always bear in mind that the reason we employ in so doing is about as dangerous for us as for our predecessors. But we may cavil at them for their errors in it, not for the attempt to use it.

We may say all this and still be proud of an ancestral policy now known as 'muddling through'. We may still admire the results of a millennium of it in the land of Burke and Morley; and when Mr. Chamberlain assures the Commons that the policies of that land have never rested upon logic and under heaven never will, we may fling up a proud cap for the intuitive experience, for the genius of compromise ... for whatever it is that the policies do rest on. But it will be better not to claim that there is a philosophy of muddling; or rather, to admit at once that there must be some species of philosophy if ever we shall muddle *through*. It will be no shame to us if we conclude that we must have some end in mind, or get nowhere; and the moment we inquire the end, we are off into political philosophy, where we shall need all of the reason we can muster, and where we cannot gracefully assail our predecessors for the use of it. In all admiration we may risk the thought that Edmund Burke was the sublimest 'muddler through' our race has borne; and possibly the only thing that ill became his noble mind was the rage he vented upon some of the men who may have helped to form it.[1]

The popular persuasion that the *Social Contract* is some species of abomination in decadence might remain unnoticed if it had not been encouraged in the masses by distinguished critics who presumably had read the book before they scandal-

---

[1] For when Burke indulges in an abstract idea on government he is very likely to give a perfect phrasing of the fundamental notion in the author whom he most reviles. 'He who gave our nature to be perfected by our virtue willed also the necessary means of its perfection: He willed, therefore, the state.' He willed the civil society without which 'man could not by any possibility arrive at the perfection of which his nature is capable'. There is no way of phrasing Rousseau better. We need not imply with Vaughan that Burke learned this from the *Social Contract*; it is enough to say that if he believes it, his main quarrel with the *Social Contract* is imaginary; but consult several similar items in Vaughan's *Political Writings* and in his edition of the *Contract*.

ized the public with a tale of its uncleanliness. A 'horrible' book, says Jules Lemaître, an 'odious' book; it 'makes one shudder'. For 'never . . . has a writer done more harm to man'. In whole or in part the thing is not only 'mediocre', 'obscure', 'chaotic', 'full of contradictions', 'extraordinary for incoherence', 'swarming with fallacies', 'absolutely unusable', 'inept', 'absurd', 'superstitious', 'tyrannical', 'paradoxical', 'nonsensical', and many other things repugnant to mere reason; but it is morally 'dangerous', 'pernicious', 'murderous', 'maniacal'. Many other interesting appellatives may be found in the twenty-four pages from which these have come,[1] and in the remainder of the book. It is a melancholy thing to know that in the flower of his fame Lemaître tacitly agreed to say these things, when he engaged to write the lectures in his volume for delivery to a select audience of monarchists, *before he had read Rousseau through*;[2] but it is a little pleasant to learn, if the story be true, that even these effusions were too feeble for his hearers, since one of the ladies present made complaint: *Monsieur, vous n'avez pas été assez injuste!* Is there any other author, old or new, whose critics are in such a state that the story could be true or that there could be a point in inventing it? But though the phrases are of genius, they are beneath further notice, and a sentence will suffice. Close your Lemaître, and open your *Contract*: do you see abomination, or the constitution of every free state in the modern world?

IV

For it is time to say that all the argument we have been hearing about sovereignty and freedom, all the demonstration of the unison of law and liberty, is only an elaborate vindication of the faith in 'government of the people, by the people, and for the people'. If it does not give a final proof that this is the one polity of reason, it has so far held its own at least in that no other polity has been proposed that most of us consider better. With whatever errors in detail, it has frankly remained unrefuted in the face of all the major criticisms here reviewed as well

---

[1] *Jean-Jacques Rousseau*, pp. 249–73.

[2] He admits it on the first page, where he also confesses that 'in the long perusal I was seeking reasons to condemn him'. He is frank enough to say he found some things he was not looking for, but also to tell what he *was* looking for (*ibid.*, pp. 1, 2).

as of some minor ones not mentioned. It is not peculiarly abusable, it is neither individualist nor absolutist, it is not irrationally rational, it is not 'decadent'. As a theory we have pretty well accepted it, and seemingly because we have to come to it when we face the problem of the state in reason.

But how well does it work in practice? And is it possible that the theory of reason will not fit a human race of waifs and strays so well as something rather more irrational? Possibly no living man is wise enough to answer that inquiry, though there are exceeding few whose minds are not made up upon it. Democracy is either something like divine right for them or it is sheer nonsense; there are very few indeed who really think of it as of a thing on trial. But the *Social Contract*, with its high abstractions all brought down into the terms of practice, is on trial to-day if ever human idea was. If we are to ask how it is working, we may well begin by asking how the other policies open to us would seem to work. There would seem to be but four of them; no more at least appear to have been offered, and perhaps no more are thinkable. Instead of giving sovereignty to the people, we may do the following things with it:[1]

1. Take it from the people and annihilate it. Give up any kind of state except the 'state of nature'. This is the proposal of the anarchist; but we need not ask if it would be desirable, because it is impossible.

2. Leave it with the people, but restrict it. This is done whenever the people agree to rule within a certain limit and to claim no power beyond it, as in any bill of rights. Their agreement may be very wise in practice, and may long endure; but the very act of making it will prove them sovereign over this and all agreements they may make; and it is impossible to keep them from revising or annulling the agreement if they think it wiser so to do. So we do not put a limit on the sovereign in this manner, but provide a way of working only. It is not a real alternative.

3. Leave it with the people, but divide it so among them that it rests in no one place. This is the familiar way of checks and balances in different branches of a government. There is little to be said against it, and our author recommends it as

[1] Beaulavon mentions the last three, doubtless omitting the first as chimerical.

another way of working. But it does not touch the sovereignty. Back of the divided powers is the power that apportions and maintains them, and that power is the only sovereign. So this too is not a real alternative.

4. Take it from the people and confer it on an individual or group. This is what most states have done, and what a number are still doing; and it is a real alternative. To be sure, a united people may depose a monarch or a group at any time, and so resume the sovereignty, for there can be no way to take this power from them. In this sense they are the sovereign by necessity. But there is a great difference between appointing an agent to administer the law that they have made and submitting to a master in agreement to obey the law that he proclaims. And therein is the true alternative.

So the four have really come to one. The first remains impossible, and the second and the third unreal; the fourth alone is of concern. The only question is whether it is better for the people to create their own law or to choose a master to proclaim it for them. One of these two things we all shall do. Which do we think will work best? Most of the men in Rousseau's time believed it best to give the power away; most of us to-day think otherwise. And we offer argument from theory and history alike. For we are no less theoretical if we are at times none too articulate, but only the more sweeping in assumption; and when we are most articulate, we are likely to be found repeating that 'Obedience to the law that we have made is liberty' and that 'To renounce our liberty is to renounce the state of man—his rights and even his duties.'[1] And in history we feel that the lessons upon monarchy and aristocracy are not alluring, even by the side of the poor lessons often given by democracy; so we have come to think there may be a better chance for a free people to seek and find their good than for a master to give up his own in their behalf. Doubtless a century is not so long nor we so wise that we can call this proof, but we incline to faith in it. We believe the theory works.

We ought to say with our author that it will not work for every people. It requires a certain wisdom and a certain public spirit. It will fail whenever people are too ignorant to under-

[1] *Contrat social*, iii. 310.

stand it or too selfish to keep faith with it. It will fail for savages or for decadents; they are better with another polity, at their own cost. But in the temperate zone of culture interlying we believe it works. We have no illusion of its working anywhere to all perfection. And we know it works exactly in proportion to the public spirit we provide for it. That will hold, of course, in any state; but we believe there is a better chance for public spirit to develop in a state which is in truth the public thing. We may leave aside scholastic jargon and say simply that the general will is nothing but the total sum of public spirit; and that it is no airy figment, but the sole foundation for a fit society. The one means to the right society is the right men, and no device of theory will avail without them.

But if the citizens must make the state, the state in turn must make true citizens. Public spirit can grow only in the exercise of it. This need leave us in no quandary as to which must come first, for the state and citizen will grow together, and will further each the other to the ends of interest to them both. Above all, the state will have the education of the individual, and a proper education is the sovereign way of making a true citizen. That is why our author gave another book to education, with a summary of the *Social Contract* for a final lesson in it. And so the *Contract* and *Emile* come into unison. The one would form a natural man to take his part in the natural society delineated in the other.

For the society would seem to be the one that will fulfil our nature. If we err in thinking it will work, we must some day try the other kind again—we must find a master, and see whether he will do better by us, after all. Reason seems to tell us to go on with our present experiment, and history to second the advice with the evidence at her disposal. But she has not finished with her testimony and deposed the whole truth. We are still so near our start toward the ideal which has here been set before us that the brief experiment so far is inconclusive. And indeed our history will always be continuing, and beginning all anew before our eyes; so it may never have a final answer for us. If we ask of history only, we may wait till it is over to discover what was right. We may have to find the answer, after all, in reason.

IV

THE NATURAL RELIGION

AT some moment in his slow climb out of brute sensation into ethical intelligence, man comes into religion. The moment is a vague one, and we shall not linger to describe it; but we know it comes to all men who reach a certain point in the ascent. Whatever comes to all of us at any point must be natural to man; so our first religion is a purely natural one.

Though there is surely greater good in it than evil, it is open to all uses and abuses. It may obviously lead us to a love and purity that we may hardly know without its inspiration, or it may carry us through intolerance and persecution into seas of blood. If it is used aright, it will finally flower into the pure love of God and man which is the noblest end that we can know; if abused, it may prostrate us before hideous deities who plague us with unimaginable torments, who bid us hate and slay our fellows, and who do all manner of evil beneath the contempt of the vilest wretch among us. According as we use it well or ill, we are prone to make our gods far nobler or far baser than ourselves. Nor is there any wonder in our doing so; striving to conceive the inconceivable, our poor imagination forges on to infinite perfection or to infinite abomination, or most commonly it grasps at some strange combination of the two.

In the terms of our author, our religion will be good or bad according as it remains natural or becomes unnatural. He would say that so long as it remains the simple effort of a soul to find out God, whatever be the stage of the inquiry, it is only one more product of our native sentiment seeking to know our highest destiny, but that as soon as it wanders from that search into contempt of any man who finds another god than ours, it has fallen in with pride and is open to all evil. All the evil in religion, as in every other thing, has been the work of pride. But there is no realm in which pride is harder to avoid, for we have found it easier to hate our neighbours for differences between their deities and ours than for almost any other reason.

Nor is there any other realm in which the differences are surer. When we strive to conceive the inconceivable, we are doomed to partial error and resultant disagreement. And since religion is our most mysterious interest, our errors in it are likely to be our greatest, while since it is our most vital one, they are likely to be our dearest. So we know no odium like the theological, no tortures fiercer than the martyr's, nor any wars more cruel than the ones that we call holy.

If our search for God could always remain as natural as was our first impulse to it, and could continue without any jealousy of our fellow-searchers, if it could be pursued in the spirit of tolerance proper to our holiest inquiry, our religion would fall into no abuse and would be wholly good for us. And in such a search we cannot but believe that we should all come to the same final faith in the love of God and man. We should come to it in due time because it is necessary to reason; and what is necessary to reason would be as natural for us in the end as what was necessary to impulse was in the beginning. So our final religion would be as natural as our first, and would differ from it only as all things in the final natural man must differ from their germs in the first one. And if we have known no such blessedness, but have strayed into our worst jealousies to please the jealous gods we have created, our only hope is still to return to reason and be led into the one religion possible under its light.

The purest of our religions has suffered terrible abuse. The pages of its history are often red. The first Christian died in agony to appease the high priests who rent their garments at what they called his blasphemy, and in the seventeen hundred years between that awful hour and the sermon of the Savoyard Vicar a multitude of men had followed to the cross or rack or flames. The Vicar might have seen a few of them, or might have been one. And to him it seemed that they had all expired for deviations from the faith which must have been fractional indeed in the sight of the almighty and most merciful God whom their tormentors were bent on vindicating. The whole history was pitiful to him beyond all utterance; the history of what man had done with his loftiest ideal was the most pitiful thing in all the world.

For to the Vicar the martyrdom of the ideal itself was more distressing than the resultant martyrdom of any individual. In his mind the abuse of all abuses had been to shroud the simple faith in veils of inessential subtlety which had all but smothered it and which had come instead to be the things men lived and died for. He felt that every martyr in the multitude had expired for something that would have been inessential to the founder of the faith, who could not have conceivably desired the death of any man for such a reason. The founder's own mission had been to clear away the veils from the law and to reveal our two great duties of love in words that all of us could understand. His simple faith had come down in turn through centuries of subtle schoolmen only to be overgrown again with mazes of speculation which the wisest man could hardly hope to thread. And the two great commandments that we love God and man had thus grown into vast *Summas* of bewildering theology and ineffable mystery, into bitter quarrels over nominalism and realism, into revolting tenets of predestination to hell-fire, into ludicrous disputes about the proper application of terrestrial water to secure celestial bliss, and into thousands of other doctrines and ordinances and rules of ceremony, vestments, postures, intonations; as into resultant hatreds, schisms, martyrdoms, massacres, and wars of extermination. The abuse of abuses had been to forget love and engender hatred over some incomprehensible immateriality such as transubstantiation or some wretched nightmare such as infant damnation—to weave a vast web of complicated dogma and then proclaim that there is no salvation outside its tangles.

Such was the Vicar's grief: not so much that the dogmas and practices were wrong, though some of them appeared abominable, as that they so often crowded out the one thing needful from our minds and filled us instead with a thousand immaterialities. The Vicar is quite willing for us to accept any mysteries that seem convincing to us and to follow any ceremonies that are reverent; only he feels that once we put such things first we have lost the meaning of religion. Some of the dogmas and rites in vogue around him were of ancient and hallowed lineage, while others were the newest of fanatical inventions. They had all been new in their day, and probably fanatical; and to the

Vicar they were all inessential. He even felt that there is no great reverence in supposing that the subtleties of the Seraphic Doctor seem much more important to our Maker, or much nearer truth, than the newfangled doctrine of some late evangelist. Whether of the twain did the will of his Father will not be decided mainly by an examination in their philosophy of Christianity.

By the side of the sacred philosophy had grown up a vast secular philosophy often at variance with it and often equally distressing to the Vicar. The two had been in constant conflict, for every reconciliation between them had been unenduring. By the Vicar's time the conflict was at its bitterest, and any further peace appeared impossible and even undesirable. For many of the secular philosophers, though some of them still wore the cleric's garb, were finally and frankly atheist and were bent on the seemingly triumphant mission of making all the world so. It would be pleasant to say that they had learned more tolerance than the dogmatists on whom they warred, but it would be hardly true. They had no power to slay and torture, but they hugged the privilege of hating and reviling; and it would be bold to argue that Holbach and his circle knew much more of love than did the cardinals and bishops, or much less of bigotry and intolerance. There was nothing very liberal in the arrogance with which they hoped to bow religion out of the back door of the world by the end of the century.

Such is the briefest introduction to the Vicar's state of mind. A Christian and a philosopher at once, if a Christian be a man who ardently believes the Sermon on the Mount and if a philosopher be one in close acquaintance with all the reasoning of his day, he is equally dismayed because the Sermon on the Mount is all but lost in immaterial subtleties and because the reasoning of his day denies the very essence of it and of all religion. And in the grievous crisis he makes one more attempt at reconciliation. To that end he is willing to clear away many a subtlety from his religion and from his philosophy alike; all of those in his religion which only hide the two great commandments, and all of those in his philosophy except the few truths which are evident or inescapable in reason. When he has done this he believes that his religion and philosophy are one again, because the essentials of religion are necessities in reason; or in terms familiar to us, he believes that the religion which had once been natural in universal spontaneity is now natural again in universal reason.

His faith and his science therefore differ from those in vogue by a notable simplicity. To reach the vital truth in both, he has had to clear away a great deal that is insignificant in each. So he came under fire from both sides; and whoever may care to measure the relative tolerance of the priests and the philosophers of Rousseau's time might well begin with their respective raids upon the Vicar.

I

Simple as he tried to make it, however, Rousseau's faith is still complex in origin. It cannot be easy to reduce reason to her inescapable verities, or possible to avoid being the heir of the ages. Calvin and Rome, science and deism, primitive Christianity and modern evangelism, are but a few of the streams of thought that poured something into the current of his natural religion. And since this was of slow and painful growth, the best approach to it will be a short sketch of his wandering course toward its formation. The sketch will tell of a boy born a Calvinist who absconded and embraced Catholicism and who grew to manhood in a deepening devotion to that faith, who meanwhile mastered enough philosophy to give him a home among its deist and atheist leaders when he came up to Paris, who then had every article of creed tried in their philosophic fire but retained enough religion to estrange him in the end from all of them, and who finally matured his faith in the *Savoyard Vicar's Profession* and clung to it for the rest of his days.[1]

In the new Jerusalem built of Calvin's genius, a child of Rousseau's day was born to a creed as definite and a moral code as rigourous as Christendom had ever seen. Even though orphaned and seriously neglected, the boy whose fortunes we are tracing could not escape a stern religious education in

[1] Pierre Maurice Masson's *Religion de J.-J. Rousseau* (3 vols., Paris, 1916) gives Rousseau's religion a more masterly treatment than any other aspect of his thought has yet received. The first volume is a history of his religious development, and our present section is based almost entirely upon it.

Scripture and catechism, in the theological argument that flourished all around him, in sermons unending but still so pleasing that one of his own early aspirations was to be a preacher, and in a score of similar influences which bore upon him like the pressure of the atmosphere. The fact is cardinal. Whatever the wanderings of his long spiritual voyage, the son of Calvin bore the mark of his religious father, not in fervour only but often in a certain obduracy also, to the end. It is an extraordinary thing that the most sensitive and tremulous of souls should have been an heir to the most inexorable of theological logicians.[1]

At sixteen the boy absconds, abjures, and enters the Catholic fold. The story is famous—how he was softened to passivity by the food and wine and blandishments of the proselyting priest at Confignon, how he was fascinated by the charms and talents of Madame de Warens when he was sent on to her at Annecy, and how he tramped across the mountains at her bidding to the dismal hospice at Turin which saw his final submission and baptism. Whatever the inaccuracies in the tale, one fact is inescapable. No one who has ever known the kind of horror of Catholicism that would be bred into the children of a city like Geneva can doubt that at some point a struggle was necessary to overcome revulsion even in a wayward boy hungry for Catholic bread. But the conversion may have been genuine enough for baptism; and at least it grew into a sincere faith in the decade following.

In the chequered months at Turin after his deliverance from the hospice, the best things recorded are the friendships of certain priests like the Abbe de Gouvon, who vainly planned a career for him, and the Abbe Gaime, who impressed him so deeply for piety as to serve long afterwards as one of the originals of the Savoyard Vicar. But the incomparable influence in the formative decade now following was that of the extraordinary woman to whose home at Annecy he soon returned. The religion of Madame de Warens was by no means so simple as to fit into a single phrase. Well into womanhood she had held fast to Pietism, a worship extremely Protestant in its enthu-

---

[1] Gaspard Vallette's *Jean-Jacques Rousseau genevois*, possibly the best of all books on Rousseau, gives a full estimate of the Genevese traits in his mind and work.

siasm, its insistence on good works rather than on formularies, and its claim of a considerable freedom for the individual conscience in the sphere of faith—doctrines far from unfamiliar to the Savoyard Vicar. From varied motives, she had then left her home and husband for a spectacular flight into the Catholic faith, and, provided with a pension, had engaged in a career of proselytism none the less sincere because she also carried over a perceptible reserve of earlier doctrine into her new creed. She accepted the essentials, or most of them, in all earnest; but maintained a certain freedom in many minor matters, and even indulged a decided taste for philosophic speculations hardly consonant with any Christian doctrine. And as is best known, she allowed herself withal a moral licence but too illustrative of the loose relations sometimes seen in her day and land between religion and morality, and of the close connexions noticeable in certain natures between devotional and amorous fervour. In a home which was a sort of outpost of the church of God, she lived the life of a humbler but very seductive Cleopatra. To forget either fact is to misinterpret the age and the woman.

Her religion and her morals became the boy's. In intimacy with her and with the priests who thronged her house, he was fortified in the new faith. The evidence abounds in his numerous ecclesiastical friendships, in his refusal of all invitations back into the fold of Geneva, in his effort to study for the priesthood, frustrated by his inability to learn in the seminary but fruitful in his friendship with the Abbé Gâtier who became the other original of the Savoyard Vicar, in his testimony to the miracle wrought by the bishop at Annecy, in the pious prayers still extant from his youthful pen, and in many other ways. But like his patroness again, he obviously kept a certain reserve of the childhood faith that had never been wholly effaced, and, more important, he maintained a certain acreage of free opinion which was to widen steadily, even while his devotion was deepening, through the study of the philosophers to whom he now betook himself in earnest.

For after repeated failure to learn in the schools, he was finally teaching himself more than most of us secure from schooling. Instead of the wide but aimless reading in which he had fitfully indulged from childhood, he now began a solid course of study leading into all the avenues of the Enlightenment, but into its religious thought especially. For his favourite authors were those who 'mingled science with devotion'.[1] These were fairly numerous; and the fact that, with the notable exception of Fénelon, they were mostly Protestant, and a number even deist, is important for the creator of the Savoyard Vicar. In Pufendorf he found a good deal to affect his faith if even more to shape his political theory. In Addison he saw a genuine religion free from fanaticism and esteeming conduct above creed, and in Addison's French emulator, Marivaux, he met with real devotion in the midst of worldly elegance. In the Béarnese preacher Abbadie he read a refutation of infidelity on grounds alike of faith and reason, in the English divine Clarke a stern if liberal argument against materialism and atheism, and in the Dutch philosopher Nieuwentyt a demonstration of the hand of God in the marvels of nature. These men were famous in the day; and among others like them for mingling science with devotion were such writers as Pluche, Claville, and Saint-Aubin, all celebrated for declaring the glory of God from the handiwork of his creation. The scene is being set for the Savoyard Vicar's sermon, and some of his articles are shaping.

If there was something liberal in these writers, there was little that was subversive; and if certain of the others were less pious, or even destined later to seem impious to our author, it was easy for him now to miss the full enormity of their scepticism. Possibly his favourite Plutarch raised some pagan questionings, and his favourite Montaigne even more. The *Essay on Man* was nearer to deism than even its author realized; while Saint-Évremond was openly sceptical, and Bayle and Voltaire militantly infidel. But the more audacious ideas of such authors were hardly reaching Rousseau yet, and at the time when he was taking Voltaire for his belletristic model he seems to have had little notion how far they had carried Paris on the way to atheism. The *Mercure de France*, which he regularly read, took care to conceal from a provincial like himself the real ravages of unbelief among the metropolitan

[1] *Confessions*, viii. 165.

philosophers. It would therefore seem that while he was learning much in liberality, he remained untroubled by the major clashes between his science and his faith, and managed any minor conflicts by the serviceable shift of keeping the two separate in his mind. He mastered a good deal of philosophy and still retained his faith. And so the budding philosopher came up to Paris a Catholic in creed and practice, though with some Protestant residue from childhood and with large liberal accretions from his recent reading, but always Calvinist in temper. He grappled with the atheists, and in the long and often doubtful struggle he had to try every item of his faith by the acid test of reason; he emerged a deist, but perfervid from the battle.

It began in skirmishes in his first stay in Paris, or even earlier in Lyons, and came to a crisis nearly ten years later with the seizure of Vincennes; but it did not reach an end until more than a decade later still, with the Savoyard Vicar. After that there is no real change or further doubt; only repetition and defence, when under fire, to the last.

The earliest skirmishes in Paris do not seem to have shaken him, for when he went off for his year in Venice he still haunted the churches and even made close friendship with the devout Spaniard Altuna, with whom he dreamed of retiring from the world to a retreat of idyllic piety. But with his ripening intimacy among the philosophers after his return to Paris, the fiercer struggle was soon under way. Whether in the squalid haunts where he met Thérèse Levasseur or in the splendid circle where Madame d'Épinay made him her pet 'bear', the next five years are surely the sorriest of Rousseau's life. In the one world he fell into a fairly prevalent crime in packing off his babies to the home for foundlings, while in the other he tacitly acquiesced in the gilded vice and corruption reigning unashamed. He would seem in no condition to withstand the sneers at religion that were common in both circles. But it was in still another group that the heavy blows now fell upon his faith. The philosophers who took him captive were illustrious for everything but piety. They had such easy mastery of the learning that was still half-new to him, such ready wit which he strove vainly to acquire, and withal such a high purpose to rid the world of inveterate abuses and intolerable oppressions, that he could not but make common cause with them. It was in the wellings out of the extraordinary mind of his bosom friend Diderot that he heard some of the strongest arguments for abolishing Christianity, and in the audacities of his intimates in Holbach's circle that he found atheism triumphant and blasphemy a reigning form of wit. And in the days when he was spending sleepless nights writing for their *Encyclopaedia*, these men naturally concluded that he was theirs in all things.

They were all but right. Under their fire the doctrine of Catholicism, with most other specific dogma, was soon swept away from him, and at times all that savoured of religion seemed about to follow. But always there was some reserve of faith, sometimes faint enough though again hotly rebellious, to distinguish him among the band; for the current of religious sentiment sprung from Geneva and nourished in Savoy had never ceased to flow, however troubled and deflected by a philosophy which was finally to clarify it. The event of Vincennes brought it to the flood again, and if it did not sweep him back immediately to a definite creed, it started a conversion and revived all the religious sentiment that was in him. The years to come are still to clarify and fortify his faith, and to place it beyond all question of endurance. The seizure of Vincennes was above all a religious experience. If it could not take him back to Rome, or more than nominally to Geneva, since he was too far gone in philosophy for either, it brought up a great force of religious feeling and a fervour almost apostolic.

For seven or eight years he remained a friend of the philosophers derided in the *Discourse* born of his seizure. They could not know, nor he, how far his conversion was to carry him; and he commonly shunned oral argument with them because he had so little gift in it. Far from being angry at his raid, they rather rejoiced in it as another triumph for philosophy. Some of them even agreed with him. For his part, he was still so far from sure of the defences of his faith that sometimes in the dead of night he would toss in despair over his failure to find arguments to meet the atheism of his friends. But as conviction cleared and deepened in his slow-working mind, his amity with them was punctuated by increasing outbursts of defiance. And because he was so dull in ordinary converse but so 'sublime or mad' when roused, the Grimms and Holbachs entered on the little game of teasing him into a temper by venting their most audacious impieties before him. We may imagine the outburst if ever Melchior Grimm, the pastor's son from Germany, slyly recounted the advice he once gave to a certain scion of nobility always to keep three mistresses 'in honor of the Holy Trinity'.[1] We know what happened when Holbach and the rest enticed a silly priest to read them his fatuous tragedy and filled his head with ironical flattery enough to ruin him. Rousseau rose in wrath to tell the priest that the fine philosophers were making a fool of him: 'Away with you! Go and tend your flock!' Holbach was so offended that Rousseau had to quit the house.[2] And there was another outburst at Mlle. Quinault's dinner, where he was goaded by atheistic levity to cry out, 'If it is cowardly to suffer slander of a friend who is absent, it is criminal to suffer it of God, who is present. And for my part, gentlemen, I believe in God! Another word of this, and I leave you.'[3] None too 'sublime' perhaps; but the signs multiply that a man so credulous and graceless will not live long in peace with the philosophers.

Though firmly believing in a providential deity as evident to reason, he had come by this anxious time to feel that his reason was so incapable of really understanding God as to make him sure of little further dogma. If some of the established dogmas seemed so irrational to him that he could occasionally call them nonsense at the very moment when he was aghast at the impieties of the Holbachians, he was far from fond of joining in the current ridicule of them. He saw small good and some danger in disproving them, and more importance in right conduct than in loud profession. His own profession at this time would have comprised very little dogma and equally little attack on it, since that too is dogma; it would have been all but confined to faith in a God of love and wisdom, and in such good works as are commended to our hearts or in sainted pages like those of the Gospel. Further speculation in theology,

---

[1] Bésenval, *Mémoires*, 1805-6, i. 272.
[2] *Correspondance littéraire*, xv. 575, ii. 504, iii. 59–71.
[3] *Mémoires de Madame d'Épinay*, ed. Boiteau, ii. 375–81.

however interesting, would have lain beyond the needful and the knowable. So he is very near his goal, for the Savoyard Vicar does little but justify the same faith and enrich its meaning. We may call it deism. And if Rousseau still called himself a Christian, he was like many a man in pew and pulpit to-day who has surrendered nearly all specific dogma with no loss of zeal for the ideal of the Saviour and the mission of the Church.

In this spirit Rousseau revisited Geneva, five years after the crisis of Vincennes, and resumed the communion of his fathers. The yoke was made easy for him, partly because he was so famous a prodigal, but partly because so many of his enlightened fellow-citizens had now come to a faith similar to his; because, as one of them wrote, 'If by having a religion we mean being upright, meek, true, and sincere, then M. Rousseau has more religion than many a man who offers incessant lip-service to Jesus without keeping his divine commandments.'[1] It was a startling thing for the world to see an Encyclopaedist kneeling in the church of Calvin; and it was important for Rousseau as well to make a public declaration of his faith, even if it meant no alteration in his creed. The act also brought him into loving sympathy with a score of Genevese divines signal for a liberal piety which aided in the next few years to deepen his convictions. For though the essential articles of his faith are now about complete, a great deal of communion with friends and books, of reverie and self-searching, of solitude, and, possibly above all, of suffering, must still come before they find the voice of the Savoyard Vicar.

This was not awakened in the dim aisles of any church, Genevese or other. The forest of Montmorency called it forth instead. Hither, to the scandal of his philosophic friends who could scarcely fancy a mental life away from Paris, he retired less than two years later. Here he lived through many of his most inspired and many of his most troubled hours. Here he was embroiled in those personal and philosophic wrangles on which we have no time to pass a judgement but which stripped him of his friends and left him an outcast in bodily and spiritual anguish. And here, in solitude and suffer-

[1] *Annales Jean-Jacques Rousseau*, iii. 203.

ing, his genius came at last to flower; perhaps no other equal genius has flowered so tardily. Its most beautiful utterance is the one in which he finally found religious peace—the *Savoyard Vicar's Profession of Faith*.[1]

This is heralded all through his life and writings in the period. In fleeing the frivolity and pomp of Paris for the rapt communion with nature which so often transported him to voiceless adoration of its Maker, he had gone yet farther than Geneva from the complacent materialism of the Holbachian band; nor would he long remain on terms with them after he had come to find the favourite reading of his fireside or wakeful couch in Scripture. Losing them, he made his chief companions of the village priests and monks of Montmorency. The writings of the period are even more explicit. The famous epistle to Voltaire avows an optimistic belief in the benevolence of God in answer to the irreverent pessimism of Voltaire's poem on the Lisbon earthquake. The *Letter to D'Alembert* is outspoken for religious faith in its attack on certain cherished principles of the philosophic party. Doctrinal digressions of great length occasionally threaten to turn the main characters of the *New Heloïse* into Vicars from Savoy. These utterances are so full and consonant, indeed, that if the Savoyard Vicar had never spoken we could easily construct his treatise out of them. Even the creed of the state religion required in the *Social Contract* is at one with the Savoyard Vicar's; for if it is accompanied by an item ill comporting with the tolerance advocated in all the other utterances, we have tried at least to show that this is not an article of faith, but a requirement, defensible or not, of social polity. To find a faith that would be requisite to reason was the main search of all these years, and no wonder if it shows in every book.

'I will seek it with all my might while there is yet time, that I may have a sure guide for the rest of my days. I am now come to mature age and understanding; already I approach the decline of my faculties. If I wait longer I shall not enjoy the full use of them in any later search, for they will have lost some portion of their vigour, and I shall do less well what I can now do to the best o fmy ability. I will seize the favourable moment. . . . Once for all I will fix my faith and principles, and for the rest of my life I will hold fast to the best that my mind may now discover.'[2]

[1] Incorporated in *Emile*, ii. 236–86.   [2] *Rêveries du Promeneur solitaire*, ix. 341.

It is the exact truth. Weighing every fact and every doubt prevailing in the age of reason, Rousseau has finally toiled, through obstacles that often seemed insuperable, to the formulation of a faith as clear and unassailable as he can make it. And having once decided on it, he holds it to his heart for the remainder of his days, but dismisses it, so far as possible, from his mind. He has done his best in speculation; from now on he will worship, but inquire no further. He will not dogmatize about his faith, for it may not be right; but he will be at peace with it, for it is as right as he can make it. In the Vicar's words he meant to utter the last syllable of it, and if controversy later forces him to repetition, he will alter no essential item of his statement. It is his whole creed. And in yet another sense he has done his best in it. The masterpiece of his pen, it may lay a reasonable claim to the same title among all the writings in his language in the century.

II

The Savoyard Vicar is not easy to abridge. So closely does he condense a doctrine growing out of centuries of thought that hardly one of his sentences can be slighted without injury. In the effort to follow him as closely as possible, it is therefore well to say that no summary will compensate for his own words.

Whatever he may owe to Gaime and Gâtier, the Vicar is of course a man in Rousseau's own image who has traversed storm and stress to reach the faith he here professes. He is speaking to a poor boy, also of Rousseau's likeness, who has fled from Geneva to Rome, changing his religion to secure his bread, and falling subsequently into various disorders and incertitudes. The Vicar utters his faith in a scene carefully chosen to inspire reverence: at sunrise on a little mount looking across a vast expanse of valley to the Alpine summits over which the rays of dawn are pouring to make all things speak the language of the Being in whose mind they dwelt before his spirit moved upon the face of the waters.

I have no learned lore for you, begins the Vicar, nor any profound reasoning; I am no great philosopher, nor can I much care to be one. (In spite of which we shall of course find him sufficient to the philosophy of his century, for he is no less of a philosopher in trying to disprove much of it.) I was once in the condition where I now find you, or in an even worse one. I too went from sin to doubt, from doubt to despair. But the state of doubt was too violent for my soul, and I struggled to escape from it through any open way.

I went to the philosophers. I found them full of arrogance and dogmatism, claiming to know everything and failing to prove anything, but evermore refuting and reviling one another. I discovered that their great aim was to glorify themselves, and that the love of truth meant very little to them in comparison. And in listening to them I was forced to the conclusion that the two great causes for our vast diversity of doctrines are our insufficiency to find the truth and our arrogant desire to believe, or to have others believe, that we have still found it. The one thing we do not learn is to be willing to be ignorant of what we cannot know. We even prefer to make up our minds at hazard and to risk believing what is false rather than to admit we cannot know all that is true. So the philosophers did but multiply my doubts without removing any of them. And I resolved to limit my inquiry to such things as I might hope to know, or such as by that token were of import to me, and to rest content in ignorance of all the others.

I was reduced to the condition of Descartes, for all things lay in doubt as I set out to find what was discoverable and undeniable. For my rule of procedure I determined to 'admit as evident all those things to which, in the sincerity of my heart, I could not refuse my consent, and as true all those which seem to derive necessarily therefrom; but to leave all others in incertitude, without denying or affirming them, and without torturing myself to fathom them when they have no useful bearing on my conduct'.[1]

But who am I to judge these things, and what is it that I call judging? That is my first question. For if I have no power of free judgement, as I am often told, if what I fondly call my judgement is nothing but the necessary product of impressions from without me, I may as well give up my toilsome inquiries, since I can by no means choose the answers. So I must first

[1] ii. 240.

look within myself to see what instrument I am employing, and how far I may trust it.

I exist, and I have senses that affect me. This is a first fact which I have no way of denying. My sensations go on within me, since they give me to know my own existence; but the cause of them lies without me, since I am powerless to produce or to prohibit them. So I exist and other things exist outside me, namely the causes or objects of my sensations; and even if those objects are nothing but ideas, they are still obviously not within me. Now all that is without me, and the cause of my sensation, I am going to call matter. What this is I have no way of knowing, and I shall therefore enter into no meaningless dispute about idealism and materialism, since these are merely different names for what remains unknowable. Yet I know that I am one and that the objects of my senses are another, for the evidence of this is inescapable.

But I find I can do more than merely 'sense' those objects. I can compare them, can note likenesses and differences among them, and all sorts of relationships. In a word, I can judge them. For 'sensing' them and judging them are not at all the same thing. In my sensation each object is separate and isolated, but in my judgement I move the objects around, transport them at will, gather them together, superpose them, and so decide about all their relations. Passive sensation could never do this. If I had nothing but sensation, I should see two objects without ever learning that they were similar or dissimilar, as I should see a number without ever counting them. I might see a big stick and a little stick, but I could never realize that one was big and the other little; I might look at my whole hand without any hope of ever counting its five fingers. If I were merely sensitive, indeed, I should have no pathway for communication between senses, and should never know a given object which I saw and touched at once to be one and the same, but should have to believe it two; and a single object impinging on all five of my senses would be five objects for me. Thus the notions of big and little, of one and two, and of all other relations, arise from something that is not sensation, even though we may produce the notions only in connexion with sensations. They are acts of what I am calling judgement.

Whatever it be called, it dwells within me, not in the things outside me. I produce it. I am not master to decide whether I shall 'sense' a thing or not, but I am master to examine more or less what I do 'sense'. I am therefore no mere passive creature, but an active and intelligent one; and in spite of any philosophy to the contrary, I pretend to the honour of thinking. (I may be but a *tabula rasa* at birth, in that I have never yet had a sensation; but for all that, I am no mere slave of the sensations when they start, for I have power to do certain things about them.)

Thus far assured of myself, I turn to look at the vast universe of matter around me. I see matter sometimes in motion and sometimes at rest, and I conclude that neither rest nor motion is essential to it. I know there are two kinds of motion—one spontaneous or voluntary, and caused by something in the thing that moves; the other merely communicated and caused by something foreign to it. If I am told that there is no such thing as spontaneous motion, I can only answer that it is inescapably evident to me, like my very existence. For I will that my arm shall move, and my arm moves, without other cause. How this happens is a mystery to me, but in vain would you disprove it by reason, for it is evident to me beyond all reasoning; though even if I could disprove spontaneous movement, I should be but the more embarrassed for the cause of all the motion in the universe. But the evidence in all this is so inescapable that whenever I see a body moving I am bound to think that it is animated or that motion has been communicated to it. My mind refuses any other possibility.

Now the universe of matter is all moving, and its motions are regular, uniform, invariable. They have nothing of the freedom that appears in the spontaneous acts of animated creatures. So the universe can be no great animal moving itself, and there must be a cause for its motion. I cannot perceive that cause, but it is necessary to my mind. I have no way of seeing the suns circling without supposing a power to propel them or to conceive the earth spinning without a hand to make it turn. Nor does it help me to know that there are certain great laws ruling all these movements, for the laws can tell me only how things move, and never why. I know that gravitation controls every body in the firmament, but the power that orders gravitation is as dark to me as ever.

Matter cannot produce motion, but can only receive it and communicate it. The first cause of it must lie outside. The more we learn of this, the more we are driven back to a will of some sort for a first cause; for to suppose a series of communicated movements back into infinity is to suppose none at all. I am therefore bound to believe that every movement not resulting from some other rises from a spontaneous and voluntary act—to believe in a will that moves the universe. This is my first principle, my first article of faith.

I admit it is beyond my understanding. How a will can move a universe of matter is as mysterious to me as how my own can move my arm. I know nothing about it, but am bound to believe that it occurs. I wish to act, and forthwith I act; to move my body, and my body moves; so I know the will by its effects, but never in its nature. My first principle is therefore obscure, but it has a meaning and embodies nothing opposite to reason or to observation; while the contrary principle is opposite to both.

If matter in motion argues a will, matter moving by fixed law argues an intelligence. The evidence is all around me— in the starry heavens circling above, in the stone falling or the leaf carried by the wind below, obedient to unchanging law. The order of the universe is as clear to me as its purpose is obscure; I cannot imagine what it is all for, but I cannot fail to see that it is all working together for ends unknown to me. I am like the savage in the old illustration when he first looks at a watch. Ignorant of its purpose, he cannot fail to admire the skill of its maker and to see that every part is fitted to work with all the others for a common end beyond his power to discover. I may as well try to believe that a set of printer's type scattered at hazard in the air happened to fall in neat arrangement to make up the *Aeneid* as to believe that the infinite order and harmony of the universe rose from some still more sublime fortuity. It is not in me to accept absurdity so manifest, though it were ten times dearer to the philosophers of my day. I therefore believe the world is ruled by an intelligence, and this is my second article of faith.

It too leaves much beyond my comprehension. Whether the world is eternal or created, whether there is a single principle in things or more, are among the questions on which I am ignorant. And what does it matter? In so far as such questions may become of moment to me, I shall strive to answer them, but until then I renounce all curiosity in problems which are only too likely to lure my pride into realms beyond my reason, but which are idle if they have no bearing on my conduct. But that the universe proclaims an intelligent ruler is indeed of moment to me.

To the Being who moves and orders all I give the name of God. In him are the will, the power, and the intelligence which the world evinces; in him also the goodness which we shall soon find necessary to those attributes. But little more than this may I know of one who is above all human knowledge. 'He is hidden alike from my senses and my reason, and the more I try to ponder him the more I am confounded. I know of a surety that he exists, and that he exists of himself; I know that my existence is subordinate to his, as is that of everything I see. I perceive him all around me in his works, and feel him within me. But the moment I would contemplate him in himself, the moment I would ask where he is or what he is, he has escaped me, and my bewildered spirit sees no more. Overcome by my own insufficiency, I will never speculate upon his nature save as the sentiment of my relation with him makes it necessary.'[1]

Having at least found the attributes in which I can conceive him to exist, I now turn back upon myself and ask what is my place in the order of his creation. I find I am a member of its highest species. By virtue of my will and of my power to execute it, by virtue of the intelligence which gives me to know and govern so much around me, I am king in my world. For not alone have I tamed the forces of inanimate nature to my ends, not alone have I discovered fire and harnessed the winds, but I have also learned what order and beauty are, what virtue is, what love and duty mean; so I am exalted above all other creatures in my ken. I would take no pride in this, for I did nothing to deserve it. I can but tenderly bless the hand which

[1] ii. 248.

dealt so generously with me. And from my first look upon my lot is born a sentiment of thanks and homage to my author.

Yet when I think of what my kind have done with all their gifts, how dismal is the contrast! Where nature offers only harmony and order, man is straying amid chaos and confusion. The very beasts are happy while their king is miserable. Evil is at large in the world of a God who is good!

But out of my very distress at this apparent contradiction is born a sublime idea of my lot. For in meditation on my nature I am constrained to find within me two diverse principles of matter and spirit, or of sense and will. The better of them frees me for the search for truth and for the love of good, while the worse enslaves me to the appetites and passions. I can feel the opposites soliciting for mastery within me. ' I will and then I violate my will, and I know that I am enslaved and free at once. I see and love the right, but do the wrong. I am now active in the use of reason and now passive in surrendering to sense; and my worst remorse, when I give way, comes from the feeling that I could have resisted.'[1] And I know I am not one, but two—I am matter and spirit.

I know all the subtle arguments in vogue to show that these are one, and that free will is illusion. The arguments do not explain what goes on in me. I feel that I am given to know the two principles by a voice within me which drowns out every argument, and I can only think of those so arguing as having closed their ears to the voice within. To me it says in no uncertain tone that I have a will superior to my body, and that when I exercise the will or give way to the body, when I conquer or succumb, I know full well whether I have done as I should or have only fallen prey to passion. I have the power to will even in moments when I am too weak to execute it. When I yield to sense I stifle the will, but when I reproach myself for my own frailty I am listening to it again; and I am a slave by my sins but free by my remorse. Only by a total depravity such as would hush all protest against the desire of the sense can I lose the conviction of my liberty.

I know the will is free only from the evidence within me, as I know so much else. I know very little of its nature. I do

---

[1] ii. 249.

not for a moment fancy it is free in every sense. Of course I am not free to will my own harm, since I cannot but desire my good. I can will only what is good for me, or what I believe to be so; but so much at least I can do without any coercion; and my freedom lies precisely therein. It surely does not follow that I am not my own master because I am not master to be another than myself. In so far I therefore believe that man is free, and animated by an immaterial soul; and this is the sublime idea which I deduce from the very evil that surrounds him. It is my third article of faith, and all the rest will soon derive from it.

It may explain the evil in God's world. All that man does freely must lie outside the mandate of Providence, and all our evils rise from the abuse of the freedom we enjoy. God does not will the evil I am free to do, but does not hinder me from doing it, whether because the harm I can accomplish is as nothing in his eye or whether because he cannot hinder me without cancelling my freedom and so leaving me in a still poorer plight. He seems to leave me free to choose, but so to restrict my powers that my evil choices cannot trouble the general order. To murmur against him for not hindering me from evil is to protest against enjoying a nature capable of good; in a word, against not being like a stick or stone. Only the abuse of my gifts can make me vile, and all my sins are of my own choosing. Take but these away, and all is good. And I need seek no further for the author of my evil, for it is I.

Whoever is omnipotent must be good. For if omnipotent, he must extend through all his creatures, so to speak, and cannot do them harm without injury to himself. He who can be all will therefore of necessity be good; and he who is good will also be just. Now if God is just, he must surely have decreed a life for us beyond the body. For if it be not too presumptuous to say so, he has given us some sort of promise of that life in making us as we are. To give us the idea and the need of happiness, and to write in our hearts the unmistakable message that if we are good we shall secure it, is equivalent, for omnipotent benevolence, to promising it to us. Yet we do not find it here below, where the wicked so often flourish while the good lie prostrate. I cannot but believe that God will keep the promise in another life. And though I have little idea what manner of life this may be, I can find no valid argument against its possibility. If the soul is immaterial, there is no reason why it should perish with the body. The dissolution of the body tells us nothing of the soul's fate. And it is altogether possible that when set free from a body with which it has been in conflict, the soul may go on in a purer and fuller life.

Whether this will lengthen out to immortality I cannot know. My finite mind will not conceive what we are fain to call infinity, and I cannot affirm or deny or really reason about what remains beyond all stretch of my imagination. I believe the soul will live long enough to satisfy justice, but who knows whether this will mean for ever? The most I can say is that whereas I can understand how the body perishes by division into atoms, I can imagine no such fate for a soul which seems indivisible; and that since I am unable to see how it can die, I incline to think it lives always. But these things are beyond me.

We shall really survive only if we remember our own past, and no doubt the memory of all that we have done in the body will one day form the felicity of the good and the punishment of the wicked. When we shall be free from the illusion of the senses to enjoy the contemplation of the truth, and when our conscience thus regains full power, the comparison of all that we have done with all we might have done will give us the measure of happiness or misery that each of us is now preparing for himself. I do not know whether there will be other sources of joy or bitterness, but these are sufficient to console me for this life and to make me hope for another. I do not say that the good will be otherwise rewarded; what reward can they desire beyond living in their true nature? Neither do I say that the torment of the wicked will be everlasting. I know nothing of it, but can hardly think it will be endless. When our carnal needs are over and our insensate desires gone, our crimes and passions must cease with them. Of what sin can we then be capable? Delivered from depraving sense, even those who have been evil must henceforth desire the good, and whoever turns to the good can hardly be for ever wretched. So much at least I am tempted to believe; but once more these matters are beyond me and have little interest for me.

From the contemplation of his works and of such of his attributes as I can dimly conceive, I have thus come in some degree to know God. But ever as my idea of him grows the grander, it passes all the power of my understanding, and the nearer I approach to the eternal light, the more I am dazzled and blinded by its brilliance. Vainly would I strive to shed all the terrestrial notions I must leave behind me if I would understand God, vainly do I strain and vex my reason to conceive the inconceivable. Even when I say that God is spirit and that my soul is spiritual, I am very near to sacrilegious terms; as if my soul and God were one in nature! Even when I say that God is the sole absolute Being, the sole Being who acts, thinks, feels, and wills of himself, and from whom we hold all our thought and feeling, all our will and life, I am but straining with ideas infinitely insufficient though already far beyond my feeble understanding. God is intelligent, but what can I know of his intelligence? Man is intelligent by reason. But the Supreme Intelligence can have no need of reason. There can be no use of premises and conclusions in a mind where all truth is one idea just as all places are one point and all times a single instant. Strive as I may to transcend my feeble faculties in the thought of God, I can but prove my incapacity to think upon him. And if by using my best reason I have caught some glimpse of attributes in him of which I still may have no adequate idea, I can but affirm these without thought of understanding them. 'In a word, the more I strive to think on his infinite essence, the less do I conceive it. But it is, and that suffices me. The less I conceive it, the more I adore it. I prostrate myself and say: "Being of Beings, I am because Thou art; to lift my soul to Thee will I meditate Thee now and for ever; and the best use of my reason is to annihilate itself before Thee." ' [1]

After thus learning something of the great verities of import for me, I have left to ask what rules I may derive from them for my own conduct if I would fulfil the purpose for which I have been placed here below. Always following the same method, I discover these in no abstruse philosophy, but find them written in the depths of my own heart in the ineffaceable characters of nature. Let us see what they say to us.

[1] ii. 257.

Which is more agreeable for us, to see men in torment or to see them happy? Which is sweeter to do, or sweeter to have done, an act of benevolence or one of evil? Who gains our hearts upon the stage, the villains or the heroes? The answer to these questions is indubitable; and it refutes every philosopher who tells us that we are naturally indifferent to anything except as it affects our personal interest, and that there is therefore no morality in our nature. If not, why do we have transports of admiration for heroic actions of the great souls of the past which cannot possibly affect our present interests? Why would we rather be Cato tearing out his entrails than Caesar riding in triumph? Surely our own interest is untouched by what happened two thousand years ago; then why have we such a horror of Catiline? What prompts us to instantaneous anger at the sight of an act of violence in the street, and to rush to the defence long before we have time for thinking? Why are we moved by the sight of a noble act to wish that we had done it? Because we hate the wicked not solely for the harm they do us, but for being wicked. Because we wish not only to be happy, but to see others happy also. Because it hurts us to see them suffer; hurts us even in our greatest depravity, for the most perverted of us never wholly loses the sentiment of pity which is natural to man. In a word, because a moral sense is part of our nature.

The moral sense has been essentially the same in every time and place. Through a vast variety of usages and customs, and under many strange and cruel cults, the world has kept about the same idea of honesty and justice, the same basic canon of morality, the same elemental notions of good and evil. Ancient cults may well have fabricated gods so hideous that here below they would have met the fate of criminals, but even when vice descended in celestial robes the moral sense of man repelled it from his breast. Men celebrated Jove's debauches but esteemed the continence of Xenocrates, just as Lucrece worshipped a whoring Venus but treasured her own chastity; and the vilest of divinities were served by the noblest of men. There has never been a time or place where it was a crime to keep faith or to be kindly; where a good man was despicable or a bad one estimable. So I conclude that in the depth of our soul there is an innate principle of justice and virtue by which we judge the good and bad. To this principle I give the name of conscience.

Only too well do I hear the clamours of philosophers against the word. 'Fiction of the nursery,' they cry; 'fallacy of education.' No such thing as conscience is native to man, and whatever goes under the name is simply planted in him by mothers and nurses, by priests and schoolmasters, who perpetually tell him what is right and wrong. Conscience is but a fruit of education. For Locke has proved to all time that there is nothing in the mind but what experience writes there, and that all our ideas are acquired from its teaching.

Now I am not going to argue that we are born with any ideas in our minds. But I would distinguish between our ideas, which are undoubtedly given us by education, and those antecedent dispositions which are quite as certainly born in us, and to which I give the name of sentiments. We do not have to be taught to desire our own good and to shun our harm, for we are so inclined by nature. The love of our own good is obviously prior to all knowledge in us, and is one sentiment that is born with us. But if man is sociable by nature, as cannot be doubted, he must also have a native sentiment of attachment to his kind. If he had no other instinct than to satisfy his own hunger, he would obviously drive away his fellows instead of flocking with them. But he loves to flock with them. He therefore has two inborn sentiments, the love of self and the love of kind. And in making some sort of peace and union between these two sentiments he encounters his first quandary in conduct. It is then that conscience is born. All this happens long before man can reason or have any idea properly so called, before he can be said to know good and evil. But to know the good is not to love it; nothing but the sentiment we are describing can make him love it. And it is this *sentiment* of conscience which is innate.

Man is therefore good by nature, and meant to grow into morality. All philosophy so far has failed to give us any other reason why we should be good. There is but one final reason, that it is our nature so to be; that we are true to our nature only as we follow our own sentiment toward perfection. We have therefore found a basis for morality. But we need not here lay down specific rules for daily conduct, for the list would be interminable. It is sufficient for the moment to have found a guiding principle. If many of us stray from it and grow deaf to the voice of conscience, it is because so much in our artificial lives tends to make us forget the language of nature which she uses. The fallacies and fictions of our sophisticated world, of which she is so wrongly said to have been born, are really her most cruel enemies, and their clarion voices often stifle her. Fanaticism even dares to counterfeit her image and to decree crime in her name. Under such betrayal she may finally resign and speak to us no more; and it will cost as much to win her back as it did to banish her. I had once grown all but deaf to her, as I have told you; and I should have gone on vacillating endlessly between good and evil, in perpetual contradiction with myself, if I had not found the faith I am now uttering to you.

I know not why my soul has been imprisoned in a body. I have not entered into the decrees of my Maker. It may be because a soul that remained free could acquire no merit, but this is only a timid conjecture. I would not murmur against degradation in the body, although I would aspire for the moment when I shall be released from it to be free and whole. In order to rise as near as I may to that state in advance, I accustom myself to sublime contemplation. I meditate the harmony of all creation, not in order to interpret it in my vain systems, but in order to admire and adore its almighty author. I lay my soul open before him, and commune with him as I may; and touched by his infinite benefactions, I bless him for all his gifts. But I do not pray for more. What could I ask? That he change the order of the world for my sake, and do miracles in my unworthy favour? A prayer so impious would merit punishment more than reward. I do not even beg him for the power to do right. Why ask for what he has already given? He has granted me a conscience to love the right, a reason to find it out, and the liberty to choose it. If I still do the wrong, it is because I so will; and to beg him to change my will is to ask of him what he asks of me—to wish him to do the work while I take the reward. The supreme prayer of my faith can be only that his will be done. And if I have another

it is that he may show me to correct the faults in these my
reasonings if they are wrong.

The Vicar pauses here, and might have closed. He has
said what he would of the natural religion and kept silence
about all others. But the boy, in perplexity among the established creeds soliciting and threatening him, asks for light on
these also. ' Tell me about revelation, about the Scripture,
about the obscure dogmas amid which I have been vacillating
from a child.'

I should have remained silent about these, resumes the
Vicar, if you had not asked, and should continue silent now if
you had any settled faith. I should not feel at liberty to shake
it. But in the anxious bewilderment in which I find you, I can
hardly harm you with the rest I have to say; nor could I well
harm the general public, which is now in a similar state.

I have told you of the natural religion, and I cannot but
think it strange that we should need another. I do not know
what else another can prescribe in moral duty, or in dogma that
is useful to man and honourable to his Maker. As we look upon
the spectacle of the creation and listen to the voice within us,
does not God say all to our eyes, our consciences, and our intelligence? What will men say more? Their revelations have
only degraded God by clothing him in their own passions, as
their dogmas have only benighted us instead of enlightening
us. To his ineffable mystery they have added only absurd contradictions, and to our susceptive spirits they have lent only
arrogance, intolerance, and cruelty ; instead of peace on earth,
they have carried sword and fire through it. I am at a loss to
see the good in this.

I have spent my faculties to find the natural religion with
which I would remain content, and if I am now to examine all
the revealed religions to make sure which is true, I shall need
some other faculty to guide me. I cannot take the word of
other men. For aside from being like myself, open to the same
truths and liable to the same errors, they are telling me all sorts
of opposite things; and there is no use in my asking them which
of them is telling the truth, for they will only keep on saying
the same opposite things. If I can therefore rely neither on my-

self nor on others I must look for nothing less than an indubitable revelation of the truth.

I am offered a revelation. I am offered a great many revelations, with an equal number of religions. Now if God is just, one of two things must be sure: either all of these religions are acceptable to him, or if there be but one of them which he prescribes and which he will punish us for not embracing, he must have given it such clear and unmistakable marks of truth that no man will be excusable for misconstruing them—no man of any time or place or station, whether European, Indian, African, or savage islander. For if there were but one true religion which we should be punished everlastingly for not accepting, and if there were a single man of good intent in any corner of the world who was not convinced by its evidence, the deity of that religion would be the cruellest of tyrants.

Yet you are asking me to say whether there is one true religion. Let us see what I must do to find out. I am told that God has spoken. To whom? To men. Then why did I not hear? He gave others the message for you. Then other men must tell me what was said; but they tell me such different things that I am back where I was at the beginning. Useless again to ask them who is telling the truth. But God protects you by manifesting the mission of his messengers. How? By miracles. And where may I see the miracles? In certain books. Who wrote the books? Certain men. But they write such different books that I am still in my first quandary. Always men! Always men to tell me what other men told them! Always more and more men between God and me!

These are the answers I receive, and if you still ask me whether they are true, I have no choice but to test and verify them all as best I may. But what a colossal labour! First I must gather all the erudition to explore extreme antiquity in order to make sure which of the abounding books of prophecy and revelation are creditable. I must find the critical insight to discern authentic from apocryphal, to deal with questions and objections, to determine whether aught has been suppressed or added, transposed, altered, or falsified, to reconcile the contradictions that remain, and to do all manner of similar things. None of these may I avoid except by taking some one's word, and I may take nobody's word because the very question you are asking me is whose word to take.

If I finally make sure of the authentic books, I must then prove the mission of their authors by examining the miracles they wrought to manifest it. Once more I must be such a master of strange tongues as to tell what is truly prophecy in them from what is mere poetic imagery; I must learn the laws of probability to decide what prophecies need miracles for their fulfilment; must know what events are in the order of nature or above it, how far an adroit man may fascinate the simple and impose even on the wise, how great and manifest a miracle must be, not only for men to believe it but for them to be damned for doubting it, and all the other things necessary to discern true miracles from false ones. Surely I cannot take for true all the miracles that simple folk the world over say they have seen, or all the contradictory religions would be right and there would be more miracles than natural events; and for that matter, the very authors who tell me that God does miracles here below assure me that the devil also reproduces them in equally attested prodigies for his own purpose, and so warn me to be on my guard. Indeed I do not know how my state could be more parlous. For even if I manage to surmount all obstacles and somehow decide that certain miracles out of the mass are genuine, I am left with the worst question of all: why a being who has the power to make all clear should choose to prove his message by a means which has in turn such urgent need of proof. But far from surmounting the difficulties, I do but tread perpetually the same vicious circle; when I ask how I may know the message is true, I am told that the miracles prove it, but when I ask how I may know what miracles are true, I am answered that I must believe the ones which the message itself certifies. Thus I prove the doctrine by the miracles and the miracles by the doctrine.

I have no way of believing that if God desires to make a thing so clear to me that I may reasonably be damned for misconceiving it, he will force me to all these labours only to leave me in such a final quandary. I know my reason cannot fathom God, but I am unable to think of God as repugnant to all reason. As for the miracles, I have therefore come to feel that the unalterable order of the universe better shows the wisdom underlying it, and to believe in God too fully to accept so many miracles so little worthy of him. And as for the doctrine, I can but think that if it comes from God it will bear the holy nature of divinity. It will at once clarify the feeble notion which our reason gives us of him, and prescribe a cult and duty consonant with such attributes as we must conceive in him. But if it teaches us absurdities and asks us to revere a God of anger, jealousy, and revenge, a God of war, a God of torments, I shall not be tempted by its travesty of reason and divinity to quit the natural religion for it. If the natural religion is insufficient, it is so because of the obscurities admittedly remaining in it. A true revelation would clear all these obscurities away; but one which only deepens them by adding irrational contradictions can have nothing to commend it.

All of this would be a mere beginning if we were going through with our question. Out of all the diverse religions ruling among men in mutual proscription, we have really been thinking of but one so far; and to be fair we should have to examine all the rest, and everywhere go through the same researches. For the firmer a conviction seems to us, the more carefully should we inquire why so many other men should fail to embrace it. But what learning we should need! What languages to conquer, what libraries to peruse! What books even unobtainable! And since the books are one thing and the practice of their doctrine is another, what travels to find out the real religions of the various lands, even of lands that print no books!

At our door in Europe we find three great religions. One accepts a single revelation, another two, and the third three revelations. Each despises and denounces the two others with blind charges of impiety and fraud. Can any fair man judge among them without first considering their evidences? But this is anything but easy. In all three the sacred books are written in tongues unknown to their present devotees. Of course the books are translated, but in our inquiry we should have to ask whether the translations are faithful, whether any such translations can be faithful. Now we might repeat that it seems incomprehensible to entrust what is all-important to an unknown tongue, to take such pains to speak and yet employ translators and interpreters, or to shut up in any book at all what every man is required to know under pain of punishment. But aside from this, how many Christians have been fair enough to ask what Judaism charges against them all the while they are denouncing it? And how would they find out if they were impartial enough to try? Not from any book, for such a book would be immediately burnt and its author thrown in chains. Not from conversation, for the few of us who can talk with the Jews will never hear their argument until they are less familiar with our cruelty and can open their minds without risking their lives. And all this is equally true of the Mohammedans. So the fairest-minded and most gifted man among us will find it very hard even to hear the evidence for the three religions nearest to us. And since two-thirds of the world lives under multifarious cults far more remote, the task of examining them all is utterly impossible.

If we are willing to be fair, we may put ourselves for a moment in the place of some one on the other side of the world who has just heard of our religion and must make up his mind whether to accept it. What can he say? You tell me that a God was born and put to death two thousand years ago in a land I never heard of at the other end of the world, and that all who have not believed this will be damned. These are strange tidings for me to accept at once on the word of a man I never saw before. Why were these events brought to pass so far away from me if it was to be my bounden duty to know of them? Is it a crime to be unaware of what happened long ago at the Antipodes? Could I divine that there was once a Jewish nation and a city of Jerusalem? You say you have come to teach me. But why did you not come to teach my good old father, and how can you damn him for dying without ever having heard? Do but put yourself in my place in all good faith, and ask yourself how I can believe all these incredible things on your sole testimony, or how I can reconcile such injustice to my father with the infinite justice of the deity you are announcing to me. In all fairness let me go and see the far country where occurred so many marvels unknown to me; let me go and find out why the people in your Jerusalem treated

God like a criminal. They did not know him for God, you say. Then how shall I know him, I who have never heard of him till now? They have been punished, you add—subjugated, oppressed, and dispersed until none of them now dare to approach the sacred city. But those who live there now, what do they say about the deicide done by their predecessors? They deny it? They do not know him for God either? Then you might as well have left the children of the first inhabitants.

What! In the very city where God died neither the former nor the present inhabitants believe that he was God, and yet you wish me to believe it, two thousand years later and two thousand leagues away! Surely you must see that before I give credence to the book which you call sacred and which I cannot read, I must at least consult others besides you as to when it was written and by whom, as to how it came down, and as to what the people of your own world who reject it give as their reason for so doing when they know as well as you all that you have been telling me. You must agree that I shall have to go to your Europe and your Palestine, and look into all these things. I should be mad to believe you before doing so.

This is what any one of us would have to say to a man bringing such marvels from the other side of our own world. It is the only rational thing that could be said. And it follows that if there be one religion only which we must accept under pain of damnation, we shall have to pass our lives examining and comparing all the various religions, and travelling through the lands where they exist. No man could be exempt, and no man could dare to take another's word. The artisan dependent on his toil, the tiller of the soil who cannot read, the demure and shrinking maiden, the invalid scarce able to leave his bed, and all men without exception would be mad to do aught else but study, meditate, argue, and travel through the world; and the whole earth would be covered with pilgrims voyaging at great expense and pain to search out and verify the various creeds and conjure forth the truth. Adieu all other occupation, for what else could matter? Yet hardly would the last survivor, though he used his time and talents to the full, find out in his old age where to fix his faith; he would be fortunate indeed if he made sure before his death of the belief in which he should have passed his life.

The picture is preposterous. But you will find no relief from it so long as you believe there is one sole religion outside of which all men are damned. Nor can you mitigate the argument, so long as you cling to that position, by letting any of your pilgrims take the word of some one else about the true faith. For the moment you do that you give up the whole position. If the son of a Christian ought to take his father's word, then the son of a Turk ought to do likewise, and so on for the rest of humanity; and there will be no one obligatory religion, but all religions will be legitimized. Thus the argument that there is a single true religion will make every man a Protestant, and thus the dogma that there is no salvation outside the Church will dismember the Church itself.

Such, my child, are the absurdities to which our arrogance and intolerance will bring us when we insist that we are right and all the rest of mankind wrong. I take to witness the God of peace whom I adore that all my speculations in these matters have been of good faith. But seeing that they were and always would be useless, I could but give them up and rest content with the religion I found written in my heart in the indubitable characters of nature. I could in no wise believe that I was obligated, upon pain of torment, to the superhuman task of fathoming the others. So I closed my books. There is one book open to all eyes, the glorious manual of the divine creation. In that sublime book I have learned to worship and obey its maker. No man is excusable for not reading it, for it speaks a language known to all men. Though I were born in an island of the sea where I never heard what men believed in the four quarters of the globe, I could still learn to know God by the use and cultivation of the faculties that he has given me, could come to love him and his works, and to do that which is pleasing in his sight. Can the learning of man teach me more?

If I were a wiser reasoner, perhaps I should come to feel the truth of revelation and its utility for those who have the fortune to accept it. But though I see arguments for it which I cannot combat, I see others against it which I cannot surmount. Between the two arguments I am unable to decide, and I neither admit it nor reject it. I reject only the obligation to admit it, for the reasons I have given; for the reason that the obligation is incompatible with a God of justice. Aside from this I remain in reverent doubt.

I would confess that the holy character of the Gospel is an argument which appeals to my heart, and that I should regret to find a refutation of it. How puny all the books of the philosophers beside it! Can it be that a Gospel so simple and so sublime was wrought by man? Can it be that he whose history it tells was but a man? What beauty and what purity in his morals! What wisdom in his teaching, and what majesty of utterance! What readiness and insight in reply to cavil! what mastery of passion! Who is the man, who is the sage, that can live and die thus? The death of Socrates in calm discussion with his friends was as peaceful as man could desire; that of Jesus in torment amid the mockery and curses of the rabble was as horrible as can be known. Socrates blesses the man who tearfully offers him the poison; Jesus prays in agony for his insensate butchers. Ah, if the life and death of Socrates are of a sage, the life and death of Jesus are of a God.[1] How can men think the Gospel is a fiction? It is not thus, my child, that we write fiction. The Gospel bears such striking and inimitable marks of truth that any man who could have invented it would have been more astonishing than its hero. And yet this same Gospel is full of things incredible, of things repugnant to reason, of things impossible for our minds to conceive or admit. What are we to do in all these contradictions? Remain always modest and circumspect, my child; silent in what we can neither reject nor understand, and reverent before the Being who knows all.

In so much involuntary scepticism I remain—a scepticism nowise painful to me, however, since it does not cloud the principles of duty on which I am already clear. Over dogmas without bearing on my conduct I can suffer none of the anxiety which others feel. I look on all religions as so many salutary institutions which provide for various peoples, in accordance

---

[1] *La mort d'un Dieu* (ii. 280); to avoid misunderstanding the fervour, we must remember with Faguet that if Rousseau had been a Trinitarian he would have written *La mort de Dieu.*

with their character and circumstances, uniform rites of public worship. I believe them all good if God is duly served in them. The essential worship is that of the heart, and all added ceremonial is a matter of variant human custom. I know well that uniformity of ceremony is a practical necessity for a given people worshipping together. And called as I am to the priesthood of the religion I profess, I therefore follow with all possible precision every rite its ceremonial prescribes, and I should suffer in my heart if I failed wilfully in a single point. I used to celebrate the mass in the perfunctory fashion that so often comes from frequent repetition even of the gravest words; but I now say it with a truer veneration. Uplifted by the majesty of the Supreme Being, conscious of my own insufficiency, and remembering that I am offering the vows of my people in the form established, I scrupulously observe all of the rites prescribed. I utter every word attentively and take care to omit no smallest point of ceremony. When I approach the moment of the consecration, I aspire to all the reverence recommended by the Church and required by the grandeur of the sacrament, and I endeavour to efface my reason before the Supreme Intelligence. Whatever be the meaning of the inscrutable mystery, I do not fear that in the day of judgement I shall be condemned for having profaned it in my heart.

Honoured by a holy ministry, though in the lowest rank, I will never do or say anything unworthy of my sacred office. I will always preach virtue to my people and exhort them to good works; and so far as I am able, I will set them an example. I will try to make religion lovable to them and to strengthen them in every tenet that is useful and obligatory. But God grant that I may never preach the cruel dogma of intolerance to them; that I may never tell them any of their fellow-creatures will be damned because there is 'No salvation outside the Church'! Whatever comes, I will not so blaspheme against the justice of God.

If there are Protestants near my parishioners, I will hold them in full charity, and will encourage both flocks to love each other and to honour all religions while living peacefully in their own. I cannot think it well to tempt any one away from the religion in which he was born; until we have more light, we are not wise enough for the responsibility. So long as a man enjoys any good faith, I shall not alarm his peaceful soul by conjuring up difficulties with which he cannot cope. But once the faith is shaken, we must save the trunk even at the expense of the branches. So it was with you, my child. Your weakening conscience needed fortifying to save it from extinction; and in order to replace it on a firmer basis, we had first to clear away the mouldering foundations on which it could no longer stand. That is why I have given you the profession of faith which God reads in my heart. You are the first to hear it, and you may be the last.

To you, in your crisis, I have opened my heart. What I hold for certain I have given you for such; and my doubts I have given you for doubts, my opinions for opinions. I have told you all the reasons for my faith and doubt. It is now for you to judge, in your own time. I would not argue with you, for argument brings heat, and vanity and obstinacy rise to spoil good faith. If you should come to feel as I do, I have one word more of counsel for you. Return to your own country, resume the religion of your fathers, follow it in the sincerity of your heart, and never leave it again. It is very simple and very sacred, and to me it seems more consonant with reason and morality than any other that I know. But whatever your decision, remember always that true religion is above all human institutions, that a pure heart is the only temple of God, that in any land or Church the love of God and man is the summary of the law; that no religion can abridge the duties of morality, that these alone are essential, that the religion of the heart is first of all among them, and that without it no true virtue can exist.

III

'Varlet crammed with inconsistencies' or 'genius of philosophic reasoning'? 'Rag of metaphysic floating in the sunshine of sentimentalism' or 'the fairest spiritual creed the world has seen'? Or simply the impassioned if broken 'cry of a soul for its God'? The clashes of criticism still abound;[1] but let us begin more pleasantly.

[1] The quotations are from: Voltaire, in one of the many outbursts written in the margin of his copy of the *Savoyard Vicar* (see Masson's edition, p. 469); Madame de

I am, and there are other things. I have sensations from them, but I wield judgement over them; in a word, I think. Thought tells me that God is, or otherwise the moving universe is inexplicable; that he is intelligent, because its motion is such; and good, because omnipotence cannot be otherwise. I am matter and spirit, and am free to choose between their ways; and the evil in the world comes from my bad choices. I shall have another life, since God is just, and it will probably be eternal; in it I shall be as happy or as miserable as my conduct here has warranted. To guide my conduct here I have a conscience to love the right, reason to discern it, and liberty to choose it. This is about all my religion: God, a soul, a life to come, a duty here; nearly all else is beyond my fathoming. Of the many established cults I am unable to say which is best, but am persuaded that God cannot require of me the impossible labour and learning necessary to find out. So I accept none and reject none; I reject only the obligation to accept, as incompatible with justice. The Gospel and the life of Jesus are the truest intimations of divinity I know. But I hold dear all religions that honour God and make for good; and I counsel every man to cling to that of his birth, for I am not wise enough to say that another will be better. Only I would not have him despise his neighbour for clinging to another. For true religion is of the heart, and is one everywhere.

To strip the faith down to this skeleton and call it Deism is, as usual, to lose about as much as can be gained by giving anything so large a single name. The Deism of Rousseau's day, rooted in the thinking of far earlier days, was only less diverse than were the various orthodoxies with which it was more or less in conflict, and to call a man a Deist was hardly to imply more than that he believed in some sort of God who might resemble anything from a watchmaker who had disposed of his product and retired from business to a loving father guiding the footsteps of his faltering children. A given Deist might be striving to be like a primitive Christian or aspiring for anointment from Holbach, or he might stand in any intermediate position. So to say that Rousseau rises out of

Staël, Œuvres, 1820, i. 63; Morley, Rousseau, ii. 279; Lemaître, Jean-Jacques Rousseau, p. 279; Masson, La Religion de J.-J. Rousseau, ii. 117.

Deism to put a crown upon its doctrine is to take only the first step in placing his religion. To do more we must look briefly at the real welter of faith and infidelity amid which it arose.

At the time when Rousseau wrote there was possibly less Christianity among thinking men in Paris than there had ever been, or may ever yet have been, in any quarter of the Western world since the establishment of the religion. Forty years earlier the mother of the Regent had written that 'There are not a hundred persons in Paris, priests included, who possess a real faith'.[1] She was speaking only of persons in the great world, of course, and even so we may allow for scandalized exaggeration. But by the time of the Savoyard Vicar so much English Deism had come over to pass under French logic into atheism that the sentence will come nearer accuracy as to the opinions of enlightened people.

In the humbler circles there was of course a good deal of simple faith. Many a parish priest was still earning a pittance by nurturing a flock in the creed of its fathers, which the flock accepted as of old. For such parishioners the Vicar is not writing. Only one in twenty-five of them could read; and the Vicar would have done nothing to alter their simple trust except perhaps to soften the intolerance with which it might be mingled. But in the higher prelacy and their followers there was another picture. There were certain learned theologians still refining upon subtleties descending from the Middle Ages and tending to eclipse the essential faith under a mass of immateriality— men who still imagined that God ruled the universe according to their little orthodoxies, men by whom the early Christians might well have been sent to the rack for heresy. More numerous were the high-born or fortunate prelates who waxed fat in opulent sinecures and flourished as courtiers, statesmen, intriguers, wits, minor poets, and men of fashion of whom no particular faith or moral code was predicable. As for the Faith, one contemporary record tells us that perhaps five or six of the French bishops still believed in God;[2] many of them certainly believed rather in Holbach. As for morals, we read that one

[1] Quoted by Taine, *Ancien Régime*, 6th ed., p. 375.
[2] Taine, *op. cit.*, p. 382.

high dignitary of the Church avoided scandal by allowing his
two mistresses to sit at his table only on unofficial occasions.[1]
This may have been exceptional, but it was possible and it has
parallels. So far as the Faith went, the Bradlaughs and Ingersolls
of that day might have been bishops, and so far as morals
mattered, the Falstaffs and the Figaros. What was the religion
of the Papal Nuncio who knelt with Du Barry's slipper when
she leaped stark naked out of bed?

To clap the pestilent Savoyard Vicar into prison was doubtless an item of it, for good form was still strong amid these
elegancies, and was ruthless indeed on any heresy that was
unfashionable. It ruled likewise over many of the lay friends of
such prelates. Polite people might well conform in season to
the popular error by going to mass 'so as not to scandalize
their lackeys, though the lackeys know that it is only for their
sakes.'[2] But otherwise the men and women of the world had
followed the prelates, or led them, over into the camp of the
materialists, where they were scrambling for the scraps from
the philosophic feast. 'Do you know what *the philosophers* are,'
asks Horace Walpole from Paris, 'or what the term means here?
In the first place, it means men who, avowing war against
popery, aim, many of them, at a subversion of all religion.'
Even Voltaire is getting to be a zealot of the last age for them.
'The *savans*—I beg their pardons, the *philosophes*—are in-
supportable, superficial, overbearing, and fanatic: they preach
incessantly, and their avowed doctrine is atheism. . . . Voltaire
himself does not satisfy them. One of their lady devotees said
of him, *Il est bigot, c'est un déiste.*'[3]

Thus had the philosophers triumphed, with a speed suggestive of the way ideas may range and conquer in the Gallic
capital. Within a century they had undermined the Faith; and
they had also gone far to undermine all moral principle save
that of gratifying our desire in the most convenient manner.
We ought to say that we are under many debts to the philosophers for clearing away immemorial errors and abuses, and
helping to prepare the better world in which we live; but alas

[1] Taine, *op. cit.*, p. 383.
[2] Quoted by Taine, *op. cit.*, p. 380, from Mercier's *Tableau de Paris*, iii. 44.
[3] Letters to Conway, 28 October, and to Gray, 19 November 1765.

that the reforms made solely in the name of rationalism should so commonly be alien to elementary morality, and that simple love and kindness should sit so uneasily in the seats so-called of reason! For the kind of reason in which these men were so courageous was about the narrowest that can be known to intellect. As it got rid of religion by simply denying anything it could not see, it abandoned all morality in the assumption that man is a machine and nothing more; and meanwhile it was as bitter against any other kind of reason as it was sanguine of its own infallibility. Man the machine has but one motive, to get all he can; for that purpose he may treat other men well when it pays, but only because it pays. That is all. Whatever pays is right.

'Pain and pleasure,' says Helvétius in a classic sentence, 'pain and pleasure are the only motives of the moral universe, and the love of self the single basis for a rational morality. . . . What other motive than his personal interest can actuate a man?'[1] And the corollary will soon be inevitable: 'Man of nature, follow thy desire, hearken to thy need; it is thy only master, thy sole guide. Dost thou feel thy veins warmed with a secret fire at sight of some charming object? It is thine; thy caresses are innocent, thy kisses pure.'[2] Such is all the morality that reason knows for thee.

For beyond thee reason knows nothing. All but thy machine is fiction and nightmare. 'If a man-hater had been bent on mischief to the race, what could he have done worse than invent the notion of some incomprehensible being about whom men would never agree but to whom they would go on attaching more importance than to their very lives?'[3] This 'Being, Esquire', this 'Monsieur l'Être' as we philosophers call him when the right people are listening, has done more harm than any other human hallucination, and can do nothing except harm. The sooner we get rid of him the better, and we shall

[1] Quoted by Taine, *op. cit.*, p. 286, from Helvétius, *De l'Esprit*.
[2] Quoted by Taine, *op. cit.*, p. 288, from Brissot, 1780. It is ironical indeed that sentiments like these, which aroused Rousseau to the pitch of his revolt, should be just the ones which the popular and often the learned mind of posterity ascribe to him above all other writers. For one example out of many of the kind of doctrine commonly supposed to have been dear to Rousseau, but really abhorrent to him, the reader might peruse Diderot's *Supplément au voyage de Bougainville*.
[3] Diderot, *Entretien d'un philosophe avec la Maréchale de* . . . ed. Assézat, ii. 513.

do it very soon indeed. And as for his Nazarene emissary, you may agree with Voltaire the Deist that he was 'a well-meaning fanatic and a good man withal, but weak enough to want to get himself talked about', or you may prefer to think with Meslier the *priest* that he was 'a vile and wretched good-for-nothing, low-born, ignorant, untalented, and awkward, who passed for nothing but a lunatic and a seducer from the moment he appeared and got people talking about him, and who was despised, ridiculed, persecuted, whipped, and finally put to death, like most of those who have tried to play a similar part without the courage or the address for it'.[1]

This should be enough to place the Vicar. If such sentiments were not universal, they were very much in fashion. The Vicar's was the single philosophic voice raised in protest. Because the religion still professed was overgrown with a theology which choked the simple faith while yet remaining mighty for intolerance, and because the philosophy in vogue was dealing death to all religion and morality, and was hardly less intolerant, Rousseau rose against them both in the name of the Faith so shrouded and of the duty so denied. In suing for peace between science and religion, he had to make many a concession to the philosophy of the day and also had to cut away many a branch from the Faith. The result was inevitable. The orthodox of our own day throw up their hands in horror at his heresy, while the unbelievers scorn him for credulity; but between the two he has a following. Even so in his own time. The Churchmen burned his book in Paris and Geneva, and the philosophers raged at it everywhere. Outcast from both groups, Rousseau nearly met the fate predicted by the Vicar for any one who should 'dare to confess God among the philosophers and also to preach tolerance among the bigots', the fate of being 'sole in his party'.[2] He was lonely enough when all his old friends left him; he was like a man who had tried to give one hand to Holbach and the other to John Wesley, only to be buffeted by both and to buffet back. But he was not quite 'sole in his party'. Many men who had been shaken turned to him as offering a

---

[1] Quoted by Masson, *op. cit.*, iii. 16, 17, from Voltaire's *Dieu et les hommes* and from Jean Meslier's *Testament* as redacted by Voltaire.
[2] ii. 286.

faith which held in reason, and their number grew. The increasing fervour led many of them or of their children back into the Church itself; and in the remarkable revival of religion which followed the age of atheism, Rousseau was the main influence in his land for the restoration of Christianity. He had been the single author of genius there to keep a religion. We may wish that it had come from cleaner hands, just as we may wish that the honest doubt of Holbach and Voltaire had come from men as honest. If we cannot choose between their persons, we may take our preference of their doctrines.

IV

'Rag of metaphysic floating in the sunshine of sentimentalism.' In whatever tone of admiration or contempt, the classic criticism of the Vicar is that he employs reason, or its semblance, merely as a halo for the edicts of his heart. The heart said, Let there be God, and there was God. The incidental reasoning has seemed variously sound to various critics— often 'glib' and 'miserably inadequate' to Morley, usually 'firm' and 'very strict' to Masson, altogether 'consecutive', upon the premises, to Höffding[1]—but it has seldom seemed disinterested to any one. In innumerable ways it has been called the handmaid of emotion. The Vicar 'tests his reason by his heart', according to Vallette, and so 'the tenets of the natural religion which he thinks are proved by reason are nothing but the voice of that inner sentiment' on which he always relies; though it is just this which gives them their great 'originality' and 'fecundity'.[2] 'Through the sentiment and not the reason does Rousseau find religion', agrees Höffding, although 'his religious sentiment is in no conflict with his reason'.[3] His idea of God may be 'lightly fenced round with rationalistic supports of the usual kind', says Morley, but it is still 'essentially the product not of reason, but of emotional expansion'.[4] After far more careful thought, Masson is in general agreement. 'A manual of sentimental truth', he says, rather than of rational conviction; for the quest is not for 'the

---

[1] Morley, *op. cit.*, ii. 271; Masson, *op. cit.*, ii. 92, 93, and *passim*; Höffding, *Jean-Jacques Rousseau et sa philosophie*, tr. Coussange, p. 131.

[2] *Jean-Jacques Rousseau genevois*, pp. 222, 224.

[3] *Op. cit.*, p. 130.   [4] *Op. cit.*, ii. 264.

truth called metaphysical', or 'truth properly so called', but only for the 'pragmatic' verity that concerns and satisfies the Vicar's heart.[1]

Without pausing to ask whether any faith is proof against these censures, whether it can be a faith if it is demonstrable, we may say at once that the religion of Rousseau is obviously open to such criticism. He admits about as much a hundred times, and with no sense of shame. Yet perhaps no one of the phrases just quoted tells the full truth about the way he sought and found conviction. We shall be wondering whether they do so as soon as we look at the grave dangers which some of the critics see lurking in such a faith.

For religion of the heart, some of them say, is simple anarchy. I will trust in my own heart, and you in yours, and every other man in his; and we shall have as many creeds and moral codes as we are men. Each of us will follow his own dear desire, with no curb in reason. 'You cannot demonstrate an emotion', says Morley, and 'a subjective test necessarily proves anything that any man desires'. So the very principle I plead for my religion is as good for any other, or against all others. 'Even the fairest Deism is of its essence a faith of egotism.'[2] Equal anarchy in morals, continues Lemaître: reliance on *my* conscience is pure 'individualism in morality', which is a contradiction in terms and no morality at all. The criticisms are so crucial that it may seem strange to find that both critics are admirers of the Vicar, and that Lemaître in particular calls his creed the fairest that the world has seen. But possibly the most terrible phrase, however intended, comes from the Vicar's most devoted student. Masson warns us that the Vicar's reasonings are just what we must expect from any anti-intellectualist. So cogent are they in their separate portions, and so fused by a single ruling sentiment, that they coax us into a sense of consistency; but ponder them well, and they fall in pieces in the light of reason. The pieces may indeed be put together in another unity; but a unity of sentiment alone, and not of reason. Once again, the heart is nearly all. And Rousseau's faith, however beautiful, is only the expansion of his own soul; so much so, in the final analysis, that 'in the paradise of

[1] *Op. cit.*, ii. 88, 89, 92.   [2] *Op cit.*, ii. 265, 276, 270.

Jean-Jacques, God himself will be forced into discreet retirement to make room for Jean-Jacques', whose swelling heart will fill it all.[1]

It is hard to disagree with Masson, but still harder to believe that any man so humble and so reverent as the Vicar can be really plotting single-handed insurrection in the skies for God's eviction and his own enthronement. In wondering how his truest friend can make a charge so monstrous, we are forced to the suspicion that for once the friend has missed the spirit and made the most of the letter; or that there is some error in the premisses or reasoning that can lead to a conclusion so subversive of the Vicar's obvious intention. And we must suspect a similar flaw in all the other phrases we have quoted if they really lead to a conclusion so revolting to the Vicar and so opposite to every word he says. It need not be a great flaw; a little rift, and logic may do the rest, as we know but too well. Give but a rift for logic, and lo! He who suffered little children to come unto him because of such is the kingdom of heaven is convicted of a plan to devote them to eternal flame by holy predestination. When our logic brings us to such passes, there is but one thing to do: look back for the rift, great or small.

There would seem to be two rifts, both in the premisses. They can scarcely be elsewhere, for the reasoning on the premisses would seem conclusive. If our hearts give us as many creeds and moral codes as there are men among us, and if we must still trust only in our hearts, we are surely on the way to anarchy. And if Rousseau would be horrified at anarchy, he must show us that one or both of the premisses is contrary to his meaning.

The first one is the easier to deal with. Rousseau does not believe that the hearts of men will speak as many languages as there are men. Each of us has a conscience, but it does not follow that our consciences are all at war; rather is it evident that they are all essentially agreed. The moral sense is one and common to us all. In the dim past when it was the sole guide to men in whom reason was as yet unborn, it spoke the same essential language to them everywhere; and interpenetrating now with reason until each controls and aids the other in

[1] *Op. cit.*, ii. 120.

coping with the complex problems of our present lives, it
speaks the same essential language still. It has no peculiar
whispers for the individual ear, but a message good for all
humanity.

Rousseau argues this from the history alike of faith and
morals. As for the faith, he feels that the inner voice has always
given man the same essential creed in the same stage of his
advance. On the whole, he thinks, the farther we go back into
religions born of simple sentiment, the nearer do we find them
to agreement, and the farther we come forward into those
admixed with speculation, the more do we find them differing.
Even the most speculative ones come nearest to agreement in
the portions where the sentiment still plays the larger part, and
are farthest from it where reflection has the upper hand. Gather
all the Christians, Jews, and Turks together, leaving out the
theologians only, and you will find them very much at one on
all essentials: God, the soul, a life to come, a duty here, and
all the rest of the Savoyard Vicar's faith. But let in the theologians, and dissension will begin over hypostasis and transubstantiation and a hundred other subtleties unuttered by Jesus,
Moses, or Mohammed.[1] And as for morals, Rousseau feels
that he need only ask whether the inner voice has not everywhere and always uttered the same basic commands—whether
there has ever been a time or place where love and benevolence
were despicable, where honesty was undesirable, or any elemental virtue ignominious. No, the voice of conscience is
essentially the same always, and its promptings will not make
for anarchy.

This is not to say that sentiment is superior to reason. It is
to compare them in no way, for they are incomparable, and
either is a poor thing without the other. Neither is it to say
that reason is bound to lead to discord. Right reason is one for
all of us, and ought finally to bring us harmony. But it is to
say that the misuse of reason is the thing which has created
most of our dissensions, and that these must not be mainly
charged against our sentiment; or that sentiment will tend to
unity, not anarchy.

If the first premiss falls, the second might remain in any form

[1] *Lettre à Beaumont*, iii. 93.

without entailing anarchy. But we cannot leave it in the form proposed if we are to understand the Vicar. Of course he does not mean us to rely on sentiment alone, and in spite of all apostrophes to conscience he has sought to make this manifest; for he is insistent on the rigid use of reason in its sphere. So much is sure; but possibly the spheres he would allot to senti-ment and reason in their joint work of ordering thought and action are still inexactly measured in the phrases we were quoting a few pages back.

The Vicar is avowedly developing a new *Discourse of Method*. He too is in a state where all things are in doubt. If more impatient than Descartes to get out of it, he is still re-solved to do so only by admitting as *evident* all things which he can have no way of denying, as *true* all things which reason necessarily derives from what is evident, and as *doubtful* all other things whatever. Now the first split between him and Descartes, if it be one, comes with the word *evident*. 'I think,' says Descartes, 'therefore I am;' I begin in intellect. 'I feel,' says Rousseau in effect, 'therefore I am;' I begin in sentiment. And Rousseau may believe that he is cutting a little deeper than Descartes in founding his existence upon simple sentience, for he goes through a considerable comparison of 'sense' and 'judgement' before he is assured that he can think. Such is the first split, *if it be one*; for in spite of all the mouths and phrases that philosophers may make, it is possible that there is very little difference between the two. It is by no means as if one of them had said 'I am a pure rationalist and therefore exist', while the other had protested 'I am just a nervous system and there-fore have being'. Doubting every other thing, Descartes can-not escape the one sure fact of his own doubt. At least he has mental processes, and therefore is; so much is undoubtable, or *evident*. Likewise doubting all other things, Rousseau comes to the same single fact which brooks no denial. He too has pro-cesses of mind, and therefore is; and this is simply *evident*. The one phrases it '*Cogito, ergo sum*', and the other might have phrased it '*Sentio, ergo sum*'. But the phrases are very much like two names for the same thing, and with a common denominator may both mean 'I have consciousness, therefore I am'.

No doubt the phrases are entirely appropriate to the temperaments in question, and no doubt one of the authors rears a system in which reason holds a fuller sway, while the other builds one in which sentiment plays a large part. The point now is only that both begin with a fact anterior to reason, or simply evident. That first fact is evident because there is no way to escape it; we may as well say that it is evident because it is evident. We are not reasoning in a circle when we say this, for we are not reasoning as yet at all. Reason has nothing to do with it. Reason can work only when she has a fact to go on, and she cannot produce the first fact because there is no prior fact to derive it from. The first fact must be something simply forced upon us. It must be an axiom to the nature of our mind. 'I am' is such an axiom.

To the blend of axioms thus anterior to reason in us Rousseau gives the name of *sentiment*. It might have saved us trouble if he had called it something else, but we must use his terms and understand them. There was a time when sentiment made up all our mental life, for we had not yet come into reason; and even now it plays a large part, for it is born earlier than reason in every one of us and continues to live beside her all our days. Self-love is such a sentiment; we seek pleasure and shun pain long before we can know why. Sympathy is another; we love our kind long before we can give a reason for so doing. Conscience is still another; we feel that we ought to do certain things long before we can have any notion of duty. It is not too much to say that 'I ought' is as much an axiom for Rousseau as 'I am'. And these sentiments, with their little host of corollaries in operation, make up our primal nature and provide reason with the axioms she has to work on when she comes upon the scene.

Rousseau would therefore agree with Morley that 'you cannot demonstrate' a sentiment, but not that it is less sure on that account. Prior to all demonstration, it is the bed-rock of all demonstration, and thus surer than any demonstrable thing. It is simply the one sort of thing in which we have no way of supposing we are wrong, and which we cannot escape except we be transformed or annihilated. Nor does Rousseau mean to be an 'anti-intellectualist' in saying this. With all his errors, he means to be the best philosopher he can, in order to refute the pestilent 'philosophists' in fashion; and he has no notion of discrediting reason in her own realm when he tries to show a realm behind it in which reason cannot live.

For with certain axioms of sentiment to go on, reason may now begin and carve out a large realm of her own. From all that sentiment provides as evident, she may derive whatever can be shown as *true*. And most of the Savoyard Vicar's faith is of her building, even though the foundations were laid before her birth. Morley is therefore rather unfair in saying that 'it is impossible to set about disproving it',[1] since all of it that rests on reasoning is open to argument; and Morley himself has gone far to disprove some of it. At any rate, the Vicar goes through a good deal of reasoning, and often of a formidable kind; and there is no chance of understanding him if we start by calling all his work a pure expansion of the heart. He endeavours to push reason to the verge of her capacity to tell him about God.

If it is not in her power to fathom God, it is at least in her duty to cope with all the argument of man. Against all human assaults on his faith, Rousseau will stand on reason; against the Archbishop of Paris or the pundits of Geneva he will be as pure a rationalist as anybody; there is no other ground on which to meet them. 'To tell me to surrender my reason' to such men, or to any men, 'is to outrage the author of it.'[2] He is at his keenest, if not at his most generous, in debate with such men, and they all came off second best in logic. But in the next breath he will say that the best use of his reason, once she has shown him all that he can dimly understand of God, is to accept annihilation before the mystery. There is no inconsistency in the two attitudes. Reason must deal with all the reasoning of man, but she must stop perforce after her first faint approach to God.

For however large to human view, her realm is but a tiny islet in the vast ocean of truth; on all that lies beyond its shores we must remain in *doubt*. The Olympic games in our little isle are ruled by reason, and what is cricket there is true; who knows what it may look like to Intelligence? The Vicar has no faculty for finding out. But he does not strain to find out, for he cannot think it matters to him. He can but think that

[1] *Op. cit.*, ii. 265.   [2] ii. 272.

nothing matters to him except what he has faculties to cope with, and that he has faculties enough for all his duty here if he will but use them well. To strain ever hopelessly beyond their reach will be but to conjure up phantoms which he can never understand but which may indeed cloud the fairly clear ideas that sentiment and reason give him of his duty here. And he means to be no anti-rationalist in confining reason to the realm where she can operate.

There is thus a little sphere for sentiment alone, a little sphere where reason enters, and an infinity beyond. But there is more to say. For in the sphere where reason enters, sentiment continues operating, and the proper interplay between them in their common realm is the problem of all morals. We have seen that we have certain sentiments prior to reason which we follow without knowing why. With the advent of reason we learn that they are wise and necessary to us, and that to depart from them is to plunge after pure phantasm and indeed to hurl ourselves upon destruction. Thus far reason validates the sentiments that antecede her, and this is why Rousseau can say that the 'rule of trusting more to sentiment than to reason is confirmed by reason herself'.[1] But in our present complications neither sentiment nor reason is alone sufficient for us. Mere sentiment is blind, and dependent upon reason to find out the right; reason is concerned alone with logical consistency, and is indifferent to the right. So a coalition between them is our only hope. And we have said that the proper coalition comes when reason validates our native sentiment as the true basis for her work of building up all the elaborate rules we need, and when sentiment remains a constant moral check upon the intellectual performance. Once reason slips from that control and seeks another basis, she will lead us only from error to error. As long as she remains responsible, she may have the privilege of lifting our blind sentiment into rational morality. She will still have enough to do.

These are not our modern terms, and may not be the right ones. We are not trying to bring them up to date, or verify them, but only to get them clear. Now if it be remembered that Rousseau is contending with a band of thinkers who proclaim

[1] ii. 242.

reason for their only deity but who too often exult in using her name to banish all idea of moral principle, to wipe out all distinction between good and evil, and to justify any indulgence of passion that does not get them into trouble, it will be evident why Rousseau fought to save a place for sentiment and to keep reason within what he thought her proper bounds. Perhaps he did not win the fight, perhaps Holbach had the better of it; if so, our world is the more dismal, though that is not an argument. But unless all that we have said is wrong, Rousseau did not do battle as a mere 'sentimentalist', and we had better keep that term for other purposes. Forget the tags, look at the men, and who is the rationalist? A Helvétius whose goddess of reason gives us the single moral rule of chasing our desire with one eye open for the policeman around the corner, or a Rousseau who may have often acted no more wisely but who mustered all *his* reason to keep reason in her proper place and save her from such obloquy? We are not going to argue that Rousseau is a rationalist; he is nothing quite so simple. We have failed only if he still appears a rag of sentimentalism.

It has taken a long while to say that the Vicar's faith is something more than sentiment, but nearly all else that need be said has been involved in the argument. The answer is that reason and religion are not co-extensive for the Vicar, but that in their common territory they must coincide. It is just because he makes so much use of reason in that common territory that he has so often been under fire. Other religions, some of them the noblest and the purest, have been put forward with almost no pretence of rational proof, and have often escaped the charge of irrationalism simply because they preferred no claim in logic. The Vicar uses all the reason he can muster, and so draws the fire. 'The Savoyard Vicar', protests Morley, 'did not believe that a God had made the great world, and rules it with majestic power and supreme justice, in the same way in which he believed that any two sides of a triangle are greater that the third side.'[1] Out of all that might be said about that statement, one thing is in place here. No religion has ever proposed God in the terms of Euclid; why single out the Vicar's for laborious indictment?

[1] *Op. cit.*, ii. 264.

Undoubtedly his reasoning is often open to argument. Undoubtedly he is far more fertile in ideas than rigorous in welding them into unity, and there are inconsistencies that a ponderer will find between the various portions of his creed. Undoubtedly some of his separate ideas come short of demonstration; the idea of the origin of evil may be the worst example, though even this reminds Höffding of the solutions offered by Plato, Voltaire, Mill, and William James, and though perhaps no better solution than the immemorial one adopted by the Vicar has yet come to the poor brain of man. Undoubtedly his crucial argument for the existence of God from the movement of the universe is only an analogy; my will can move my body, and there must be a heavenly will to move the heavenly bodies. This is nothing but analogy, and will not do; though if it were in point, we might ask what any Holbachian found except analogy to drive him to the opposite conclusion, or what else any man can find; what Morley found, for instance, to warrant a belief that the soul is 'only a function of the body'.[1] Undoubtedly the Vicar is sometimes too eager for an argument to scrutinize it fully. So in many a point he fails to prove his faith. Who indeed has proved it, or its contrary? In all the tomes of theology, in all the libraries of doubt, how many books are better?

There is probably no one new word in it. An argument so old had left none to be said. There may be a profound originality, for all that, of the kind that has no need of novelty; and the fact that it always takes many a century of thinking to make ready for originality brings us to our last point. In certain phrases Rousseau has been thought to imply that his natural religion might have come to birth in any man at any time—in the primitive savage or the Parisian philosopher. Of course we know this is not true, and that man had to pass through animism, magic, superstition, revelation, Christianity, Catholicism, Deism, and many other things before producing a Savoyard Vicar. And of course Rousseau knew it too. 'Though I were born on a desert isle. . . . I could come to know God. . . . if I used my reason.' Maybe so and maybe not, and it depends a little on what is meant by *knowing*; but the most

[1] *Op. cit.*, i. 81.

infatuated primitivist, and Rousseau is no such person, is well aware that a lone man on a desert island cannot reason with Helvetius. Rousseau found it hard enough to cope with him. And this means that the natural religion may come to men only when they have reached a certain stage of reason and experience, that it is the latest of religions to develop and the heir of all the others, and that it is still waiting for more reason and experience to perfect it; or once more that the natural man is not our first brute forbear, but the last man whom we are travelling on to be.

BIBLIOGRAPHY

AN adequate bibliography of Rousseau would require another volume. Everything that has been written on him since 1905 has been listed and reviewed in the annual *Annales de la Société Jean-Jacques Rousseau*, and an index has been provided in the volume for 1926. For the main treatises prior to 1905 we may refer to E. Asse, *Bibliographie de J.-J. Rousseau* (no date), and to Gustave Lanson, *Manuel bibliographique de la Littérature française moderne* (1914). As there is no exhaustive bibliography, so there is no full and critical edition of our author.

The few items in the following list are among the most valuable at hand—(A) for the general biography and criticism of our author, and (B) for a fuller treatment of the topics that have come before us in the successive chapters of the present book.

A. GENERAL

Henri Beaudouin, *La Vie et les Œuvres de Jean-Jacques Rousseau*, 2 vols., 1891.
Louis Ducros, *Jean-Jacques Rousseau*, 3 vols., 1908–18.
Émile Faguet, *Vie de Rousseau*, 1912.
John Morley, *Rousseau*, 2 vols., 1873; revised edition, 1878.
Gaspard Vallette, *Jean-Jacques Rousseau genevois*, 1911.

B. SPECIFIC DISCUSSIONS

1. *Of the Fundamental System:*
Émile Faguet, *Rousseau Penseur*, 1912.
Harald Höffding, *Jean-Jacques Rousseau et sa Philosophie*, tr. Coussange, 1912.
Gustave Lanson, *L'Unité de la Pensée de Jean-Jacques Rousseau*, in *Annales Jean-Jacques Rousseau*, 1912.
2. *Of the Educational Doctrine:*
Gabriel Compayré, *J.-J. Rousseau et l'Éducation de la Nature* (no date).
Francisque Vial, *La Doctrine d'Éducation de J.-J. Rousseau*, 1920.
3. *Of the Political Doctrine:*
Georges Beaulavon, *Introduction* to the *Contrat social*, 2nd edition, 1914.
Bernard Bosanquet, *The Philosophical Theory of the State*, 1910.
G. D. H. Cole, *Introduction* to the *Social Contract* in *Everyman's Library*.
Edmond Dreyfus-Brisac, edition of the *Contrat social*, 1896.
C. E. Vaughan, *The Political Writings of Jean-Jacques Rousseau*, 2 vols., 1915, and an edition of the *Contrat social*, 1918.
4. *Of the Religious Doctrine:*
Pierre Maurice Masson's *Religion de J.-J. Rousseau*, 3 vols., 1916, supersedes all prior discussions.

INDEX

Reference is here made to the more important names and topics mentioned. For convenience the main topics are grouped under *Rousseau*.

Abbadie, 120.
Addison, 120.
Aeneid, 130.
Alcibiades, 48.
Alexeieff, 69 *n.*
Altuna, 121.
amour de soi, 12, 13 *n.*, 17.
amour-propre, 18.
Aristotle, 1, 103, 105.
Asse, E., 165.

Bayle, 86, 120.
Beaudouin, Henri, 165.
Beaulavon, Georges, 93 *n.*, 110 *n.*, 165.
Bésenval, 123 *n.*
Bosanquet, Bernard, 165.
Bradlaugh, 151.
Brissot, 152 *n.*
Buffon, 39.
Burke, 2, 102, 103, 105, 106, 107, 108.

Calvin, 117, 118, 124.
Cato, 136.
Chamberlain, Austen, 108.
Claville, 120.
Clarke, Samuel, 120.
Cole, G. D. H., 165.
Compayré, Gabriel, 165.
Condorcet, 25.
Correspondance littéraire, 123 *n.*

D'Alembert, 125.
Dante, 65.
Darwin, 91, 107.
d'Épinay, Madame, 7 *n.*, 35, 121, 123 *n.*
Descartes, 107, 127, 158.
Diderot, 7, 122, 152 *n.*
Diogenes, 31.
Diogenes Laertius, 29 *n.*
Dreyfus-Brisac, Edmond, 69 *n.*, 165.
Du Barry, 151.
Ducros, Louis, 165.
Dunning, W. A., 2.

Encyclopaedia, The, 69, 121, 124.
Essay on Man, 13 *n.*, 120.
Euclid, 107, 162.

Faguet, Émile, 2, 146 *n.*, 165.
Fénelon, 35, 120.
Fleury, 35.

Gaime, Abbé, 118, 126.
Gâtier, Abbé, 119, 126.
Godwin, 25.
Gouvon, Abbé de, 118.
Graffigny, Madame de, 35.
Grimm, 35, 123.

Helvétius, 35, 152, 162, 164.
Herodotus, 62.
Herostratus, 31.
Hobbes, 11, 14, 91 *n.*, 93, 101.
Höffding, 2, 154, 163, 165.
Holbach, 116, 121, 123, 125, 149, 150, 153, 154, 162.
Hugo, 13 *n.*

Ingersoll, 151.

James, William, 163.

Kant, 3, 29.

La Fontaine, 48.
Lamb, Charles, 65 *n.*
Lanson, Gustave, 2, 68 *n.*, 165.
Lasserre, Pierre, 3, 5 *n.*, 32, 68 *n.*
Lemaître, Jules, 3, 31 *n.*, 32, 102 *n.*, 109, 149 *n.*, 155.
Levasseur, Thérèse, 121.
Lisbon Earthquake, 125.
Locke, 35, 91, 93, 137.
Louis XV, 90, 91.
Lowell, 2.
Lycurgus, 78, 80.

Marivaux, 120.
Masson, P.-M., 117 *n.*, 148 *n.*, 154, 155, 156, 165.
Mercier, 151 *n.*
Meslier, 153.
Mill, J. S., 163.
Mirabeau, 101 *n.*
Montaigne, 35, 120.
Montesquieu, 81, 91 *n.*, 105, 106.
Morley, 2, 103–8, 149 *n.*, 154, 155, 159, 160, 162, 163, 165.

Newton, 104.
Nietzsche, 21.
Nieuwentyt, 120.
Nourrisson, J.-F., 3, 32.

Pietism, 118.
pitié, 13.
Plato, 37, 91 *n*., 105, 106, 107.
Pluche, 120.
Plutarch, 62, 120.
Polybius, 62.
Pope, 13 *n*., 120.
Pufendorf, 120.

Quinault, Mlle, 123.

Rabelais, 35.
Racine, 13 *n*.
Rollin, 35.
Rousseau, dissension over his meaning, 1–3; reasons for it, 3–6; his 'return to nature' not a retreat to savagery, 7–8; but an advance into the culture proper to the character of man, 8–10; definition of this character, 11–17; self-love, 12; sympathy, 13; in how far man is good by nature, 13; conscience, 14; its interplay with reason, 15–16; how man becomes unnatural, 17; pride, 17–18; how it differs from self-love, 19–20; the remedy for pride, 20–1; the 'return to nature' simply the renunciation of pride, 21; natural and unnatural culture, 22–5; perfectibility, 25; presupposes some form of freedom, 26; the three main forms—independence, 27; civil liberty, 27–8; moral liberty, 28–9; happiness, 29; incidental contradictions of this doctrine, 30; misinterpretations of it, 31–2; its essential unity, 32; its main applications — to education, government, and religion, 32–3.

The natural education, 34–68; sources, 35; some irrelevant objections, 36–7; the three kinds of education, 38; the four periods, 38–9; problems of infancy, 39–42; the two main dangers, slavery and tyranny, 40–1; both unnatural, 42; the evil of artificial stimulation, 42; the proper freedom for a child, and the proper control, 43; how they may be reconciled, 44–5; the two kinds of dependence, 44; the way in which a child should not be dependent, 45; reliance upon force rather than reason, 45–6; the 'negative education', 47; some of the things a child should not be taught, 47–50; the correction of faults, 50; in how far they are 'natural', 51–2; the positive education, 52–4; the kind of reasoning possible for children, 52–3; portrait of a natural boy at twelve, 53–4; studies from twelve to sixteen, 54–60; how to

choose them, 54–5; utility the test, 55; curiosity the motive, 55; natural and unnatural curiosity, 55–6; proper stimulation, 56; suitable subjects and methods, 56–7; the first studies of the social order, 57–8; and of the boy's place in it, 58–9; the approach of reason, 59; final studies in the social and moral realm, 60–4; expansion of sympathy in adolescence, and its rational cultivation, 60–1; a reckoning with the world of man, 61–2; history, art, literature, the humanities, 62–3; politics, 63; ethics and religion, 63–4; a contrast to this system, 64–5; further irrelevant objections to it, 66–8; the real question, 68.

The natural society, 69–112; the evolution of the *Social Contract*, 69; different from the other works, but not incompatible, 70; a continuation of the *Discourse on Inequality*, 71; summary of the *Contract*, 72–90; an agreement the one basis of legitimate society, 72; the terms of the agreement, 72–3; the Social Pact, 73–4; the sovereign, 74; definition of the *general will*, 74–6; the four conditions requisite for it, 76–7; definition of the law, 78; liberty and law, 79; every lawful state a republic, 79; the law-giver and his province, 80–1; definition of the *government*, 81–2; the three main kinds—democracy, aristocracy, monarchy, 82–5; no society eternal, 85; how its dissolution comes, 85; and how it may be deferred, 85–6; other topics of the *Social Contract*, 86; the state religion, 86–9; an alleged inconsistency, 89; contrast of this system with the systems then in power, 90–1; its sources and its originality, 91; illustration in the idea of the Social Pact, 91–3; the crucial argument that true law and liberty are one, 93–100; objections to the system—that it is abusable, 101; or too individualistic, 102–3; or too absolute, 102–3; or too theoretical, 103–8; or simply 'subversive', 108–9; the final question on the system, 110; the alternative to it, 110–11; and the verdict so far, 111–12.

The natural religion, 113–64; what the term means for Rousseau, 113–14; the final religion may be as natural as the first, 114; abuses on the way to it, 114–15; theology and science in Rousseau's time, and their relative intolerance, 116; his effort to reconcile them, 116–17; his own religious history, 117–

26; early Calvinism, 117; conversion to Catholicism, 118; growth in the faith, 118–19; induction into philosophy, 119–21; battle with the Parisian philosophers, 121–4; conversion of Vincennes, 122; return to Geneva, 124; his maturing creed, 124–5; its final utterance, 125–6; summary of this, 126–48; I exist, and other things exist beside me, 128; I compare and judge those things, and therefore think, 128–9; their action demonstrates a will, 129–30; and an intelligence, 130; that intelligence I call God, 131; I am matter and spirit, and enjoy a certain free will, 132; and my evils come from the abuse of my freedom, 133; omnipotent intelligence must be just, 133; and justice argues another life, 133–4; I can know but little of God, 135; but may know all that is of import to my duty, 135; basis of this duty laid in my own nature, 136–7; conscience defined and demonstrated, 137–8; worship and prayer, 138–9; the problem of revealed religions, 139; a rational choice among them impossible, 140–5; and if impossible, not obligatory, 145–6; the holy character of the Gospel, 146; the question of ceremony, 146; tolerance, 147; a summary of the law, 148; relation of this doctrine to Deism, 149–50; and to the current creeds and practices, 150–4; objection to its 'sentimentalism', 154–6; the provinces of sentiment and reason in Rousseau, 156–62; lapses in the argument, 163; its comparative value, 163; the natural religion, like the natural man, is of the future, 163–4.

Saint-Aubin, 120.
Saint-Évremond, 120.
Saint-Lambert, 7.
Saint-Pierre, Abbé de, 35.
Sallust, 62.
Seillière, Ernest, 3, 32.
Socrates, 27, 146.
Solon, 78.
Staël, Madame de, 148 n.

Tacitus, 62.
Taine, 150 n., 151 n., 152 n.
Texte, Joseph, 5 n.
Thales, 3.
Thucydides, 62.
Turgot, 35.

Vallette, Gaspard, 32 n., 118 n., 154, 165.
Vaughan, C. E., 3, 33 n., 69 n., 85 n., 101 n., 102, 108 n., 165.
Vial, Francisque, 165.
Vincennes, 121, 122, 124.
Voltaire, 1, 32, 120, 125, 148 n., 151, 153, 154, 163.

Walpole, Horace, 151.
Warburton, 86.
Warens, Madame de, 118, 119.
Welton, James, 68 n.
Wesley, John, 153.
Windenberger, J.-L., 85 n.

Xenocrates, 136.

Zeno, 29.

DATE DUE